MULTICULTURALISM
UNITED IN DIVERSITY
A ROMANIAN PERSPECTIVE

A Study by Irina Budrina

IRINA BUDRINA

MULTICULTURALISM
UNITED IN DIVERSITY

A ROMANIAN PERSPECTIVE

CORESI

PUBLISHING HOUSE

WWW.CORESI.NET

Cover design: Leo Orman
Cover illustration—source:
https://pixabay.com/photos/horezu-pottery-organic-colors-985765/

ISBN: 9781096352570 (KDP Print)

For further information on this book, please contact *CORESI Publishing House*: coresi@coresi.ro.

www.coresi.net
www.ePublishers.us
www.LibrariaCoresi.ro

"It is precisely because of the cultural diversity of the world that it is necessary for different nations and peoples to agree on those basic human values which will act as a unifying factor."

Aung San Suu Kyi
1991 Nobel Peace Prize

The purpose of this book is to combine a series of articles on intercultural communication, focusing on practical aspects that will help you to deal with your Romanian business partners as well as with partners from other countries, while bridging the cultural differences between them.

CONTENTS

A VOYAGE OF DISCOVERY

Irina Budrina not only knows what she writes and talks about, but she is, as they say, walking her talk. Born in Russia, having traveled all over the world, with an MBA in Japan and a Ph.D. in Romania (REI, ASE) she has been living in Romania for the last 12 years.

The present book is, therefore, based on her very rich and significant encounters with people and organizations in various parts of the world and mainly in Romania.

You are reading a book which is a voyage of discovery and learning about our own and other cultures. Leadership, intercultural communication, cultural dimensions, cultural values, and gender issues in business and beyond business are just some of the discussions you are going to be part of through Irina Budrina's knowledgeable and skillful guidance. This is a book to enjoy and to reflect upon.

Professor Mariana Nicolae, REI (ASE)

Multiculturalism—United in Diversity: A Romanian Perspective

In today's world, exposure to other cultures has become a symbol of increasing globalization processes. Many people leave their home area to go on a voyage of discovery and learning about other cultures that affects their original cultural identity.

Interactions with multiple cultural settings and globalizing transformations have affected the world over the past twenty years and increased opportunities for communicating almost instantly across previously built barriers.

The needs of the 21st century demand citizens that are culturally sensitive and internationally focused, with an orientation toward the future rather than the past. Cultural Diversity is in it.

The concept of multiculturalism offers a new orientation toward the future.

"Multiculturalism is a system of beliefs and behaviors that recognizes and respects the presence of all diverse groups in an organization or society, acknowledges and values their socio-cultural differences, and encourages and enables their continued contribution within an inclusive cultural context which empowers all within the organization or society" (Caleb Rosado, 1997).

The essence of multiculturalism is the ability to celebrate with the Other in a manner that removes all barriers and brings unity in diversity. Multiculturalism pushes us to look upon the Other not as a potential enemy but as a profitable partner.

Managing diversity is an ongoing process that unleashes the various talents and capabilities which a diverse population brings to an organization, community or society, so as to create a wholesome, inclusive environment, that is safe for differences, enables people to reject rejection, celebrates diversity, and maximizes the full potential of all, in a cultural context where everyone benefits.

Multiculturalism, as the art of managing diversity, is an inclusive process where no one is left out. Diversity, in its essence, then is a safeguard against ethnocentrism (making of one group as the norm for all groups).

No cultures should be verbally and/or physically attacked based solely on the negative meaning given due to biological, cultural, political or socioeconomic differences (such as gender, age, race/ethnicity, political party, class, education, values, religious affiliation or sexual orientation The motivating factor for such attitude is fear, arising out of ignorance of the other culture, which is different from your own.

Multiculturalism should be the only option open to educators, leaders and administrators in an ever-increasing culturally pluralistic environment. Today's diverse student populations and workforce is simply not going to go away, but increase. This is the direction of the future multicultural, multiethnic, multilingual communities. And effective leaders are recognizing it. The art of managing diversity is thus of great concern to all persons charged with the responsibility of overseeing the work of others.

Multiculturalism, then, may very well be part of an ongoing process which enables people to become world citizens—persons who are able to transfer their own racial/ethnic, gender, cultural and socio-political reality and identify with humankind throughout the world, at all levels of human needs.

The concept of multiculturalism itself

• allows to explore the meaning of culture and how cultures operate, sharing the basic values across cultures, it promotes an "awareness and appreciation" of your own culture and the cultures of others;

• helps to promote mutual understanding and a sense of belonging within and across different communities in which people are located, and an ability to engage with a variety of other communities through meaningful cross-cultural communication at local, national, regional and global levels, and more successfully interact and engage across these levels;

• values the experiences and different cultural backgrounds and creates a learning resource in a positive manner for developing skills, knowledge, values and attitudes needed to participate actively as a critically informed member of society: local, national, regional and global ;

• affirms the right of all people to access important learning strategies and resources;

• provides an educational framework that is relevant and responsive to all needs, despite the varied experiences, knowledge and backgrounds.

Requirements

Basic needs are sensitivity and self-consciousness: the understanding of other behaviors and ways of thinking as well as the ability to express one's own point of view in a transparent way with the aim to be understood and respected by staying flexible where this is possible, and being clear where this is necessary.

It is a balance adapted between three parts:

1. knowledge (about other cultures, people, nations, behaviors...),

2. empathy (understanding feelings and needs of other people), and

3. self-confidence (knowing what I want, my strengths and weaknesses, emotional stability).

Cultural differences

Cultural characteristics can be differentiated between several dimensions and aspects (the ability to perceive them and to cope with them is one of the bases of intercultural competence), such as:

- Collectivist and individualist cultures;
- Masculine and feminine cultures;
- Uncertainty avoidance;
- Power distance;

• Monochrone (time-fixed, "one after the other") and polychrone (many things at the same time, "multi-tasking") aspects;

• Structural characteristics: e. g. basic personality, value orientation, experience of time and space, selective perception, nonverbal communication, patterns of behavior.

Improving Intercultural Communication

It is essential that people research the cultures and communication conventions of those whom they propose to meet. This will minimize the risk of making the elementary mistakes. It is also prudent to set a clear agenda so that everyone understands the nature and purpose of the interaction. When language skills are unequal, clarifying one's meaning in four ways will improve communication:

1. avoid using slang and idioms, choosing words that will convey only the most specific denotative meaning;

2. listen carefully and, if in doubt, ask for confirmation of understanding (particularly important if local accents and pronunciation are a problem);

3. recognize that accenting and intonation can cause meaning to vary significantly; and

4. respect the local communication formalities and styles, and watch for any changes in body language.

5. Investigate their culture's perception of your culture by reading literature about your culture through their eyes before entering into communication with them. This will allow you to prepare yourself for projected views of your culture you will be bearing as a visitor in their culture.

If it is not possible to learn the other's language it is expected to show some respect by learning a few words. In all important exchanges, a translator can convey the message.

1. Bridging the differences: intercultural communication in business

In today's world, exposure to other cultures has become a symbol of increasing globalization processes. Many people leave their home area to go on a voyage of discovery and learning about other cultures, which affects their original cultural identity.

Where the cultures meet

Let's imagine that somebody has asked you to dance and you are moving on the dance floor with your partner in the belief that you know this dance. But it takes you a few steps to realize that something is wrong. Your movements do not match your partner's movements and, as a result, you both do not follow the music and each other's expectations. Your partner's rhythm is different from yours and you feel that you are often about to step on each other's toes.

But you do want to dance together, and neither of you leave the dance floor and you both take the initiative to find a solution. Your body is super-attentive in the attempt to find steps that will allow you to move together with the music. Finally you both succeed in creating a pattern of a joint dance. It isn't the dance that you both first expected and probably not the one that your partner imagined either.

This situation on the dance floor is very similar to the Intercultural Communication where doubts and misunderstandings arise because parties have different views and expectations of what should happen. The response you get may be different from the one you expect, and it makes you uncertain about the other party's intentions. If a cross-cultural environment is to be constructive and fruitful, both parties must bring their cultural intelligence into play and this is very similar to what happened during dancing.

Intercultural communication has become a very important part of our life. Globalization is rapidly breaking down our vision of a world with well-defined national, cultural and linguistic boundaries. Not surprisingly, Intercultural Competence has taken on an importance that no one could have imagined even

20 years ago. We've shifted into a new mode of living where transnational contact is almost a daily occurrence. The very nature of Intercultural Communication—different languages, behavior patterns and values—pushes us to avoid assumptions of similarity and to stimulate appreciation of differences.

Thus, intercultural skills—the ability to understand the values and beliefs behind behavior and reconcile them with your own—are basic, necessary tools in today's world.

Cultural diversity in business

Culture and cultural differences have a greater influence on business effectiveness than we think and it is therefore important for companies to develop the Cultural Intelligence (CQ) of their employees. As organizations become more global, mergers and strategic alliances become more common, developing the skills to get the best from different cultures become a necessity rather than an option. Innovation, knowledge sharing, and creative problem solving demand collaboration across boundaries of different professions, job functions and organizations, and these activities depend on people's ability to work with other people who think and act differently from themselves.

The cultural challenge faced by companies 20 years ago was often simply to prepare individuals to go abroad and work and negotiate effectively in a foreign national culture ("Do's and Don'ts" training). But today international companies are faced with a much more challenging cultural complexity or diversity.

The challenges and problems of culturally complex organizations cannot be solved using the thinking of past generations. We need to develop new mindsets and models. We need to see differences in a new way, where interdependence is a given and where working with differences is a competitive advantage rather than an obstacle.

Cultural Intelligence (CQ) is the ability to act appropriately in situations where cultural differences are important and the ability to make you understood and to establish a constructive partnership across cultural patterns.

Bridging the differences

Bridging the differences can be achieved in several ways:

Culture management in an organization—advising the management on how to improve collaboration among people who think and act differently and how to successfully handle the increasing cultural complexity. This is highly relevant to prevent problems and create good performance in cross-national collaboration, in M&A processes, in innovation processes and in cross-disciplinary projects. The company can go further in this path and create Cross-Cultural Capital Management within HR Department.

Leadership development—designing training programs and advising managers of cultural complex groups in cultural intelligent leadership. Developing managerial skills to bridge differences in groups and to release the synergy arising when diverse approaches meet. This is relevant for leaders of international groups, of research and development departments, of innovation projects, of cross functional teams and of strategic HR development.

Analysis and evaluations. Evaluations of strategies and outcome in the field of intercultural collaboration and/or diversity management. Analysis of the organization's ability to bridge and benefit from the relevant differences in the company based on the unique CQ model.

Managing diversity. Revitalizing the diversity strategies and activities in the company. Do we achieve the outcome we wish and in which we have invested resources? Are we working with the right groups of people? Do we have a powerful coherence between our diversity strategy and our activities? Do we work with the most effective questions and do we use the most relevant tools helping the company to energize and focus on the next steps.

2. Workplace hurdles: different cultures working together

Different nationalities working together, different cultures mixing in the working place could lead to a tough combination, especially for the leader of the team. The following story involves British, Indian and Colombian colleagues. What do you think could have happened if any of these people in the story were replaced with Romanians?

A team of young engineers from an UK University had to work on an R&D project called "Environment friendly cars in the future." The team consists of five British and four Indian guys and a Colombian woman, who is the leader of the team. The project should be completed in six months and the first draft with some tests results should have been sent to the University supervisors one week before the Christmas. It was planned to be sent but...

The team is going through a rough path and no results have been achieved so far. Indians want to work only with Indians and want to give most of the benefits to their friends, because they have been working together before in other projects. Everyone wants to make sure that their own ideas are put into practice instead of others. The way that everyone approaches and understands the main concerns are different and very few are actually concerned with the deadline. Indians and British people have different working habits, a different perception of time, a way of talking to people, even a different way of using mobile and land phones during meetings. Given all these, where do you think this team will be in 6 months?

Culture is a concept of multiple meanings. It is a practice shared by people within a community, the filter we use to interpret our existence and direct our actions. Our own culture is something that makes us feel at home in our place of work, in our country, our family, among the colleagues of the same profession, and in our ethnic groups. Culture is what we say and do together with other people in ways which distinguish us from other groups. Within our own cultural community we take culture for granted and do not think about it.

When misunderstandings arise between people of different nationalities it will often be explained with reference to the cultural differences between them, because it is so obvious that they speak different languages, perhaps dress differently and have different body languages and ways of greeting and talking together.

As long as we are within our own culture, we use our autopilot because we are moving in a known environment where routines and ways of acting and speaking are automatic habits. It is easy to make ourselves being understood by others, and we have no problem understanding what's going on.

But as soon as we enter a different culture, the autopilot must be deactivated, and we have to engage manual control and pay more attention as we are in a situation where we are not quite certain what would be the right or wrong thing to do or to say. We have to become aware that we are wearing our cultural glasses and that others are wearing their cultural glasses and experiencing things the other ways.

For example, the different ways in which national cultures experience the distance between two people. When a person from Sweden and a person from Spain are having a conversation during a reception, one notices how the Swede is slowly backing away in order to increase the mutual distance. The Spaniard experiences big distance as a weak contact which may be about to be broken and the Swede experiences short distance as insecurity and a feeling that the other person is very pushy. But when the Swede meets Japanese, however, it is the Japanese person who will be backing around the room.

Coming back to our example about a team of engineers, let's see which cultures we are dealing with: Colombian, British and Indian.

Question: What should we recommend the team leader (a Colombian woman) to do with the other members of the group? How can she make them work together?

Some hints about these cultures:

Indian managers feel that they are treated as subordinates rather than partners in their relationships with UK businesses and are subjected to prove and to demonstrate their professional competence and expertise. UK managers are also viewed as "one-dimensional," "mechanistic" and caught in a short-term transactional mindset, whilst Indian managers emphasize longer-term relationship building to get strategic benefits.

Indian managers also experience a rigid approach to time management that influences business results. To them, centralized authority within UK corporate culture is inflexible in responding to dynamic business approaches.

Colombians tend to communicate in an indirect and subtle manner. It is important not to offend others and always to be as diplomatic as possible. Meaning is conveyed through non-verbal forms of communication and often "yes" or "maybe" are preferred to "no" to avoid losing face and maintain harmony. Hierarchy is an important part of Colombian business culture and should be respected whenever possible.

Most decisions are made from the top by the senior members of staff, though often opinions and consensus is sought from subordinate employees. In Colombian business culture, cultivating close personal relationships and building trust are considered vital components for a successful working environment.

What do you think would happen if any of these team members were to be replaced with Romanians?

3. Romanian women leading a cross-cultural team: what are the challenges?

In the previous article we discussed the challenges that the leader of the team of engineers–a Colombian woman—had to go through. The mixture of cultures made this unique experience a bit spicy—five British and four Indian specialists were not mixing well, in fact the results of the projects showed that there was no team established at all. Now let's see what things would look like if the leader of the team were a Romanian woman.

A woman from Colombia with a diplomatic business culture had to develop a strategy how to work with two different groups at the same time: the Indian one, based on "family" long-term relationships and a British one, with the inflexible culture in respond to dynamic business approaches and "one-dimensional," "mechanistic" and a short-term mindset.

What would happen if the leader of the team is replaced by a Romanian business woman?

Women in Colombia can be very often assigned to the positions of power, leading businesses and usually at the same professional level as men. Women-leaders are very proud of their professional achievements, experience and knowledge.

Women leaders in Romania are an interesting phenomenon. An increasing number of women are setting up successful businesses in Romania, overcoming barriers and building their credibility inside and outside their organizations. In Romania women entrepreneurship tends to become a force in the economic development. Women make 51, 2% of the Romanian population and cover 47.6% of the total active population. Consequently, women represent a readily available pool of potential entrepreneurs in diverse fields: trade, industry, tourism, advertising, IT and communication and real estate that each Romanian region can leverage to improve its economy.

Which cultural business values in Romania can be useful in our case?

Relationships are very important in the Romanian culture and women are very in that, in business a lot of time can be spent on building trust by talking about personal issues, interesting events, etc. They tend to use personal relationships to solve work problems.—Perfect match for our Romanian Leader!

In general Romanians are risk takers. And they will work hard to close a deal once everyone is on the same track. They are actually more open with for-eigners than with each other. But even though they are skilled negotiators, they often show little knowledge of Western experiences, particularly with regard to speed, urgency or integrity. When a deal is concluded, every-thing should be put in writing, witnessed by decision makers and the competent experts. Plus an approval from the senior person in the organization.—A bit heavy for the decision-making process in our project?!

Romanians are not punctual in general. They are comfortable with ambiguity where the Westerner wants final clarity.—Are the deadlines of our project in a risky situation to be postponed even further?

What is more important that Romanian business women have demonstrated willingness and ability to adapt and to learn.

Here I would like to refer to David Livermore's book "Leading with Cultural Intelligence: The New Secret to Success" published in 2009 by Amacom in 2009 and put more stress on Cultural Intelligence demonstrated by women in Romania.

When speaking about cross-cultural leadership in general Livermore shows that: "its challenges go beyond an occasional misunderstanding." They strike right at the core of whether or not we can successfully meet our performance objectives. This is where cultural intelligence (CQ) comes in. It helps us effectively adapt our leadership strategies when working outside our own culture.

Cultural intelligence is a set of capabilities and skills that enables leaders from outside a culture to interpret unfamiliar behaviors and situations as though they were insiders to that culture.

Rather than expecting individuals to master all the norms, values and practices of the various cultures encountered, cultural intelligence helps leaders develop an overall perspective and repertoire that results in more effective leadership. For example, in culturally unfamiliar situations, sometimes other people's behavior and perspectives seem somewhat bizarre and random.

Those with high CQ have the ability to encounter these types of confusing situations, think deeply about what's happening (or not happening), and make appropriate adjustments to how they understand, relate, and lead there."

There are four major capabilities, according to David Livermore ("The Cultural Intelligence Difference", Amacom, 2011), that can also be thought towards developing our overall cultural intelligence:

The Drive: "What's your motivation for this assignment? Showing interest, confidence, and drive to adapt cross-culturally. The Drive is the leader's level of interest, drive, and energy to adapt cross-culturally."

The Knowledge: "What cultural information is needed to fulfil this task?" Understanding cross-cultural issues and differences. "Knowledge refers to the leader's knowledge about culture and its role in shaping how business is conducted."

The Strategy: "What's your plan for this initiative? Strategizing and making sense of culturally diverse experiences. Strategy is the leader's ability to strategize and plan when crossing cultures."

The Action: "What behaviors do you need to adapt to do this effectively? Changing verbal and nonverbal actions appropriately when interacting cross-culturally."

What an exciting time to be involved in cross-cultural leadership! We have the opportunity to learn from people from a wide array of cultural backgrounds. The challenges of global leadership can be disorienting, and experience and intuition alone are not enough. CQ offers us a pathway toward enhancing our own effectiveness and competitive edge in multicultural and global contexts. And more importantly, it allows us to treat one another with a greater degree of respect and dignity."

4. Doing business in Romania: main cultural values

Romania has often been labeled as one of history's greatest survivors. With a past of invasions and occupations, Romania has recently undergone dynamic social and economic changes and joined the EU in 2007. While the country attempts to leave behind its communist past, present day attitudes and traditions still reflect this part of its turbulent history. Modest attitudes and behaviors coupled with Orthodox Christian beliefs reflect their simple-minded and down-to-earth mentality that has been shaped by years of hardship.

Though they may appear abrupt or unreceptive at first, Romanians are considered among the friendliest and hospitable people in Europe with big hearts, a unique sense of humor and a strong cultural heritage. Understanding this is the first step towards successfully doing business in Romania.

Key concepts influencing the process of doing business in Romania

Relationships—As a family-focused society, Romanians depend heavily on relationships with others. Romania's history of invasions and occupation has created an environment where it takes time to get to know other people. Once a relationship is formed, however, it will be a long-term one based on loyalty and trust. This carries over into the business world, where outsiders are often treated very formally until there has been time to get to know them and establish a relationship. Romania's communist-controlled past has created a culture in which the group is more important than the individual. Relationships are therefore a vital part of the Romanian business culture and must be developed in order to succeed.

Religion—The majority of Romanians are members of the Romanian Orthodox Church, in fact they make up the second largest population of Orthodox Christians anywhere in the world after Russia. Though their religion was suppressed under communism, it has always played an important role in shaping the way they live. Romanians are very family oriented and communal and place a lot of importance on births, deaths and marriages and on their relevant Orthodox celebrations.

Identity—Romanians have experienced centuries of turbulent and difficult times but have made it through to become an emerging presence in Europe. They are proud of their country and particularly of their national heritage. As a result, they tend to be sensitive about cultural and political matters that concern their country but are always thrilled for any opportunity to share Romania with others.

There is **a strong hierarchical system** in place, with delegation coming from the top down and decisions are rarely questioned or challenged by those of a lower rank. Most business dealings are very formal and senior members of the group are given the most respect and privileges. Responsibility and position are clearly defined. Those with authority command a higher level of respect which is often reflected in the decision-making process and use of titles and formal greetings.

How do all these cultural values influence the business relationship between the expat-manager of the company and a Romanian team? Let's analyze the following example.

Olivier Marsely, a Dutch consultant, has recently moved to Bucharest to work as an auditor for a multinational corporation. He has no problem with opening a local bank account, but the bank's policy is that for the first six months he can have only debit card and not a credit one.

Coming back to his office, Olivier asks his assistant, Claudia Popescu, to monitor his account, prioritize his expense reports, and quickly process transactions with the finance department to cover the debit card's balance. Claudia agrees to take personal responsibility for this.

Two months later Olivier faces his worst nightmare: his debit card is refused when he tries to pay for his hotel in Barcelona. Humiliated and angry, he calls Claudia in Romania and asks her to take immediate action, which she does by convincing the company's accounting department to intervene.

Olivier's confidence in Claudia is shaken as he believes that she has not fulfilled her responsibilities. Complaining to one of his Indian colleagues, he is advised to dictate and monitor Claudia's work habits more directly. Frustrated, Olivier realizes that his own cultural orientation for collaboration will not allow for what he perceives to be "draconian" measures. He also realizes that he does not know how to motivate his

Romanian colleagues, like Claudia, to take more responsibilities for their tasks.

What do you think the expat manager should do in this case?

P.S. Many countries and nationalities are represented in Romania today.

The Asians have tolerated for centuries of playing second fiddle to the West, now they intend to reverse the situation. In industries such as textile, garments, shoes, toys and plastics the West has no chance to compete, not even in the future. In high-tech industries, especially consumer hardware, the West is already threatened by Malaysia, Thailand, Korea and China and Taiwan. In this situation the West's most effective weapons have to be dynamic leadership, vision, psychological skills, willingness to innovate and clever use of their democratic institutions.

The globe's biggest economies: the US, Japan, Germany, Britain and France have been particularly insensitive to their handling of intercultural issues. The very size of their national economies pushed them to assume that they continue with one way of doing business. The US went its own direction having roots from many nationalities and Japan failed to understand multiculturalism because of both geographical and mental isolation. Germans are more advanced on intercultural issues, being frank, honest and consistent. They just lack the delicacy to understand those who do not meet their standards.

Small European countries learned long time ago the rules of the game. They adapted to them, which means they aspired to multiculturalism. Dutch, Belgians, Finns, Swedes, Danes and Swiss, and to a lesser extent Greeks, Hungarians, Czechs, the Baltic states and Norwegians, have studied and achieved a certain degree of empathy with the cultures of more powerful countries. Poles, Turks and Slovenians are beginning to go down to the same track. Canada is an outstanding example of a successful and consciously multicultural society.

Almost all of the mentioned above nationalities can be met today in Romania for different business reasons.

In the 21st century, with multinationals and conglomerates expanding their global reach, corporate governance and international teams will learn a lot about leading multicultural enterprises and work-forces. The new impetus provided by fresh managers from Asia, Russia, Poland, Hungary, East European states, Latin America and Africa will change notions of leadership as will the increasing number of women in management positions.

5. Leadership style—how does culture influence leaders?

The leadership style is another area where cultural intelligence is required and where local cultures play an important role. The style of leadership valued in the Netherlands is, for example, a weakness in Romania, where authoritative leadership is seen as a strength. On the same note, the qualities of a good leader in the US would not necessarily work in Central and Eastern Europe.

Once I went to a company's regional office in Prague to join a two-day meeting with all of the company's mid-level managers from Eastern Europe. After all the ups and downs of the two-day meeting the company's regional director asked me who among the group middle-managers I considered to be the most promising up-and-coming leaders.

Without hesitation, I named three individuals who struck me as having "leader" written all over them. He laughed and said, "I thought you'd say that. Their charisma and initiative would probably be a huge **asset** in the United States, but it's a **liability** here."

He went on to tell me whom he thought were the most promising leaders—individuals: the Romanian, Bulgarian and the Czech, who had barely hit my radar. Two years later one of the individuals he identified was the new regional director and performed with excellence.

Cultural intelligence is also needed to address the challenge of recruiting, developing, and retaining cross-cultural talent. Up-and-coming leaders in emerging economies, like Romania, have many options at their disposal and they're seeking firms and executives who demonstrate culturally intelligent practice.

Executives should recognize the need to recruit the right personnel because 16 to 40 percent of all managers given foreign assignments as expatriates end them early. Nearly 99 percent of these early terminations are the result of cultural issues, not job skills. The cost of each failed expatriate assignment has been estimated anywhere from EUR 200,000 to more than EUR 1.2 million when you include expenses associated with moving, downtime, and a myriad of other direct and indirect costs (housing, schools, medical costs, etc).

Leadership style is an area where cultural intelligence is necessary to lead across different cultures. Just as individuals possess varying views and beliefs about preferred styles of leadership, cultures as a whole have varying preferences for certain leadership approaches. A participative leadership style, where the hierarchical pyramid is flat, where managers involve others in decision making was viewed as an essential way of working among most Dutch leaders and organizations. However, this same style was viewed as a weakness among many firms and leaders from Romania, where authoritative leadership was perceived as a strength.

The point here is to see the importance of having the knowledge, motivation, and flexibility to enact the appropriate leadership style in any given situation. A competitive advantage, increased profits, and global expansion are central to why many of us are interested in cultural intelligence; however, most of us would readily agree we're also interested in behaving in a more respectful, humanizing manner to the people we meet throughout our work.

Cultural intelligence can help us become more benevolent in how we view those who see the world differently from us. The desire to treat other people with honor and respect doesn't automatically mean our behavior comes across as dignifying and kind.

Managing a diverse workforce—a major test of leadership.

The task of managing a diversified and dispersed workforce at home and internationally is one the of the major tests of leadership.

Nearly 90 percent of leading executives from sixty-two countries named cross-cultural leadership as the top management challenge for the next century (The GLOBE study of 62 Societies).

Fostering good communication and building trust have always been two most important issues in leadership, but learning how to do so among a culturally diverse staff is a whole new challenge.—The main road to go for both the Dutch manager and his Romanian colleague from the previous case that you can read here.

It's impossible to master all the norms and values of each culture, but effective leadership does require some adaptation in approach and strategy. The most pressing issues executives identify as Cultural Intelligence are to understand diverse customers, manage diverse teams, recruit and develop cross-cultural talent, adapt leadership style and demonstrate respect/empathy to the local culture.

Human resource policies, motivational strategies, and performance reviews may need to be adapted for various cultural groups represented among team members. There is a need for leaders who can help teams form a local identity while still retaining the values of the organization as a whole.

Cultural intelligence is needed to achieve the right blend of flexibility and rigidity, which means "to embrace the local culture, but not to make any retreats on your values. One will get respect from the locals, if one shows understanding for the local culture/religion/behavior, but equally respect will be gained if the locals can learn something useful from you. It is a two-way avenue, where best results and great working atmosphere is created when locals and expats are learning from each other" (from our reader, Romanian by origin, who has spent eight years as a senior manager in Holland, Germany, USA and Japan).

These five reasons for cultural intelligence—understanding customers, managing personnel, recruiting talent, adapting leadership style, and communicating respect—are the most consistent reasons identified by leading executives across the world.

6. The emergency tool kit: developing a set of skills for multiple cultural situations

"Think global while acting local" is hard to implement, that's why a high rate of failures in assignments abroad is a constant statistic. But what happens when the situation doesn't allow a foreigner too much time to research and learn about the culture of the country's he or she is headed to?

In our previous story we talked about the authoritarian leadership style in East European countries (Romania was among them) vs. the participative style brought by the Western cultures leadership model. What is really expected in these countries is not necessarily for the boss to be a dictator, but rather that he/she exercises enough authority to direct people who are used to more authoritarian forms of leadership.

Dealing with people from many cultures is complicated when you need to adapt to each one.

Let's say you are arriving in Romania in two hours, so there's little time left to read up on Romanian culture right now. What should you do? Our busy lives simply don't allow us to become cultural experts about every culture with which we work.

Well, cultural intelligence offers a more promising and realistic approach. According to researchers Maddy Janssens and Tineke Cappellen's study of global managers ("Global Managers' Career Competencies", 2008)[1], a more broad-based approach for orienting professionals is needed.

Their study puts the emphasis on Cultural Intelligence like developing an overall repertoire of skills and behaviors that one can draw on when dealing with any cross-cultural interaction rather than expecting any leader to master all Do's and Don'ts of each culture.

Here is a story of CEO from Germany about how he applied his Cultural Intelligence (CQ) for an assignment in Romania:

"When it became clear I was going to be responsible to lead our work in Romania, I knew I needed to

---

[1] Career Development International, Vol. 13, Issue: 6, pp. 514–537

develop my understanding of Romania's historical and cultural background. It would not be wise for me just to rely on a general understanding of cultures to do my work effectively. But I also wasn't starting from zero. Even though I had never been to Romania nor spent any time studying the culture, my personal trainings on CQ helped me to know what kind of information to find and which questions to ask.

My previous experiences abroad and understanding of some cultures like Russian, Bulgarian and German didn't keep me from making mistakes. Our mistakes can be one of the greatest ways to grow our CQ. In fact, part of being more culturally intelligent is embracing the idea that cross-cultural conflict is inevitable and provides an opportunity for personal and professional growth."

The primary emphasis of the cultural intelligence approach is to develop a skill set that can be applied to all kinds of cultural situations. Although some initial reading and training can start your growth in CQ, we should continue to add more and more information to our repertoire for culturally intelligent leadership all through our career. The four-step model, according to David Livermore—drive-knowledge-strategy action, that we talked about in one of the previous stories, can be highly recommended.

Acculturation is a two-way street. That means that the foreign leader must also make efforts to assist the local people in understanding not only his/her style but the style of the organization or culture that he/she represents. Then give the local employees tools, skills and understandings to be better managed in that context as well. In such situations the synergy created by these efforts of mutual acculturation can create a sense of accomplishment and satisfaction among all involved.

The inevitable question to be asked here whether Cultural Intelligence is a matter of nature or nurture. Indeed, some personal traits like "openness" or "extrovert" can be positively correlated to high CQ. However, through learning and interventions everyone can become more culturally intelligent. And just because someone might have natural talent at flexing his or her behavior in cross-cultural situations, it's no guarantee he or she will be a culturally intelligent leader. Just as having natural genetics for running doesn't mean you'll be a marathon runner without training, the same is true here. It takes effort and work, but anyone can develop and nurture CQ.

P.S. An Inside-Out Approach is another step on the way to develop your CQ.

We have to move beyond behavior modification approaches where we pretend to be respectful and move toward becoming leaders who genuinely respect and value people from different cultural backgrounds. All the diversity awareness programs and creative cross-cultural simulations are pointless if we don't actually change the way we view people from within.

Getting people to use respectful language is a good start. But something more is needed.

One foreign company developed a diversity training program for its Romanian office in order to help employees to deal with the cultural differences. But thousands of Euros and lots of diversity training workshops had changed little.

Only through a more in-depth analysis showed that the CEO of the organization, a former U.S. Marine, was extremely prejudiced against local overweight employees. He viewed a local overweight employee as an evidence of an undisciplined, lazy worker. The CQ approach with an emphasis on the personal attributes of leadership may have revealed this problem sooner.

Becoming culturally intelligent doesn't imply turning our backs on our own cultural backgrounds and preferences. But it does mean we have to do more than simply change the way we talk to our colleagues who look different from us, whether that's a difference in size, gender, color, or otherwise. And we have to go beyond merely planning a diversity-training month once a year. The entire way we view one another may need to be transformed.

Cultural intelligence is a transformative model of cross-cultural behavior and leadership rather than a model built primarily on behavior modification strategies.

7. Cultural preconceptions: French and Romanians at the merger table

In a meeting of people of different nationalities, parties will notice the different practices first. But in a problematic meeting like the one in the following example, the different perceptions of self and pre-conceptions of others become important, and will lead the parties to interpret the same practice differently. What do you think about the situation below, which involves French and Romanian professionals sitting together at the merger table.

Culture is like a tailwind on a bicycle path. We notice the wind only when we change the direction and feel, all of a sudden, that the wind goes against us. We are unaware of our culture until we meet something different, we take it for granted for what it was until then.

A cultural encounter is a communication situation where differences between the participants are felt at least by one party to be culturally determined. It may be a meeting, a job interview, a spontaneous dialogue, a training situation, a video conference or a telephone conversation. What is interesting about cultural encounters is not the cultural differences as such but the importance which the parties attach to the culture and the cultural differences in the situation.

A cultural encounter can be planned when a multi-disciplinary project group has been established for the purpose of solving a problem and finding a solution, or when a new foreign manager –an expat— wants to introduce more informal knowledge sharing in a foreign brunch. The cultural encounter can be predictable when a new group of colleagues of different cultural backgrounds have to work together. It can also arise spontaneously in a situation where a topic suddenly triggers differences among participants.

A meeting of different points of view and backgrounds holds a large positive potential for the new way of thinking when we look outside our normal frames and leave old habits behind. A company intending to adjust a new product for its customers in different countries may, for example, can establish a group which includes multicultural people who know and understand customers behavior in these countries, people with commercial expertise in different fields (like advertising and marketing), and people with the knowledge of necessary technology and production.

In a described above meeting of people of different nationalities it is different practices that parties will notice first, but in a problematic meeting like the one in the following example, the different perceptions of self and preconceptions of others become important, and will lead the parties to interpret the same practice differently.

Deputy Manager of a Romanian Industrial company was highly respected and popular for his achievements and attitude towards workers and colleagues. He had been working in the company for many years starting his career straight from school, completed his internship as a metalworker in the engineering workshop, moved on his career path to the level of a floor manager and gradually worked his way up through the hierarchy completing personal education at the same time.

He was appointed as a Project Leader by the President of the company to merge with a French company which showed high interest in the Romanian company's activities and financial results.

The project group consisted of several people from both companies. The group members had a first meeting and during this meeting they introduced themselves by names and experiences in this field so that their expertise could be used in the best possible manner.

The French members of the group presented themselves with abbreviated titles and university degrees in engineering science, which did not mean so much to the Romanian members of the group. The French managers were clearly embarrassed and confused finding out that the Romanian Project Leader had started his career as a metal worker and had no university degree. His opinion was not counted as an important one by the French managers. Some of his practical examples were met with silence from the French side of the table.

After coming back to the headquarters the French group complained about him being appointed as a Project Leader. They argued that by the appointment of the non-academic manager of the Romanian company failed to treat the merger with proper respect and priority.

The deputy manager felt he was treated with disrespect and misunderstanding. His competences were questioned and he felt uncertain about fulfilling his responsibilities as a Leader of this group.

Obviously there two different patterns with respect to what was required to make a managerial career in Romania and in France. These practices had their roots in the different national cultures, but most probably were reinforced by two companies' own histories. Plus some differences between engineering community's sense of pride and status compared to the metalworkers, and the two professional groups perception of each other.

And a concept of a team should be observed in both cultures. The French one can be described as a collection of specialists chosen for their competences in a given field under the command of an unequivocal leader.—Who was questioned in our case!

Romania has a collectivistic culture where people are used to work in groups and team-spirit has been developed for many years. Romanian people are more open with foreigners than with each other. But they will work hard to "close a deal" once everybody is on the same track.

In France professional relationships between colleagues are founded more on rivalry than collaboration. This begins in the highly competitive school environment, which is based on getting over a series of ever higher hurdles.—Remember formal introductions with titles and University degrees?

Learning to collaborate to solve problems is not an educational tool.

In business, competitiveness is fostered by strong vertical hierarchies. Far from refreshing, people find it disconcerting when others do not compete. They will not wait for a group consensus before taking an initiative. To those from more participative cultures (like in Romania) this can appear deliberately provocative.

The French culture, especially in business, is based on personal contacts. Personal relationships are regarded as important for their own sake. Something similar to the Romanian culture. Can it be a solution in our case? Should people from this team, both French and Romanians, meet in an informal atmosphere? What is your advice? How should we make people with two different patterns work together?

8. Collaborating and communicating across genders

By understanding cultural differences and similarities, one can develop ways to communicate and collaborate more effectively across genders. The cultures of men and women, like other cultures, are complex, given women and men's great variety, diverse backgrounds, and personal histories. Take the following example involving a foreign manager and his female subordinate from Romania.

The world is filled with diverse cultures in which people form groups in order to survive and succeed in a specific environment. Some cultures people are born into and others they choose to enter. Given this variety of possibilities is it realistic to speak of a Culture of Men or a Culture of Women? Traditionally, we look at men and women as subcultures within ethnic or national cultures. However, some people believe that gender cultures are the fundamental starting points around which many of the essential values of a culture are formed.

Every culture offers guidelines on the appropriate ways to be "feminine" or "masculine." And men and women are expected to behave differently. In some cultures these differences are multiple and deep, in others they are fewer and smaller, but in all cultures gender differences exist.

Masculinity and femininity are cultures, just as our national or ethnic cultures. They are often first cultures, and may affect us even deeper than other parts of our cultural upbringing

We are labeled as "female" or "male" at birth. Like all values, they are sometimes creative and productive, and sometimes in need of adaptation to the fresh demands for human survival and success as environments and social circumstances change. Like all values, they can easily become stereotypes and block understanding, rather than starting points for deeper comprehension of each other.

It is important to remember that all women or all men within any nationality or ethnicity will not hold the same values with the same intensity, or exhibit the same behaviors as a result of the values they hold. When we speak of gender cultures, it is important to use the information as a starting point for dialogue and discovery, not as a fixed definition of "how we are as men and women."

Core Women's values

Collaboration. Collaborative behaviors include seeking to involve others in decisions, and acknowledging others people's experience and contributions.

Nurturing. Women easily become nurturers in work settings as well as other areas of life. They often anticipate others' needs, and do things for them without being asked.

Group/Family. In work settings, a woman is frequently the one who suggests or conducts team-building activities-both formally and informally.

Relationship. Women nurture relationships to achieve personal, work, social, and political goals. Things get done through relationships. A woman may even take more work home because relationship issues take up a good part of her formal working day.

Harmonious Communication. Because relationships are important to survival and success, women often communicate in a less direct manner to avoid disrupting relationships by embarrassing or angering the person with whom they are communicating.

Core Men's Values

Courage (Hero). Man is a brave hunter, an adventurer, a scout, who explores the unknown and comes back with provisions for those for whom he is responsible.

Loyalty (Leader-follower-comrade). A man is faithful to his commitments, sticks to his principles, performs his duties, is loyal to his friends, and true to his word. He observes and enforces the rules, respects his leaders, and understands the responsibilities of rank and file.

Making & Doing (Worker, artisan). He makes things and makes things happen. He should be active, creative and productive even if his business or work is not physical (e.g., politics, teaching, etc.). He should master his trade and his tools. He minds the business.

Play (Sportsman). He is brought up to compete and win as a preparation for his roles in work and life. He is to develop sportsmanship, camaraderie, and team spirit.

Knowledge & Wisdom (Philosopher-poet). A man should be rational, logical, and curious, and prefer sure thinking and clear speaking. He takes things apart in his mind or with his hands to see how they work.

Men and women can be quite adaptable. They can learn to speak and behave in new ways in order to succeed in different situations. This is not always easy, and may cause emotional pain and social consequences. For example, when women start to behave in more "masculine" ways in an attempt to succeed in leadership, management, or other roles, they may feel confusion and stress. The people around them may also have difficulty coping with the change, which may add to their stress. They may have a sense of guilt because they do not see themselves acting in a womanly way, or because they feel they are giving up their own values in order to "fit in." One woman executive said, "I have been very successful in the business world. And when I look at myself in the mirror, I often grieve the loss of my original values and female self." Such a feeling of loss-of-self happens often to both men and women as they adapt from one culture to another.

By understanding cultural differences and similarities, you can develop ways to communicate and collaborate more effectively across genders. The cultures of men and women, like other cultures, are complex, given women and men's great variety, diverse backgrounds, and personal histories.

Some values can give you clues to how men and women might view the world, feel about situations, and live their lives. While no one can foretell what another person thinks, will do, or will say, values tell us something about what to expect, and give us clues about how to work with people from a culture different than our own.

Case

Hans Van der Strok is a Department Head of an engineering architecture at the International Construction company in Romania, a company specializing in solutions for bridges and over-water transportation devices, whose clients range from municipalities to military engineering. Simona, who graduated from a Polytechnic University with honors in engineering, was eagerly hired about a year ago by this Company and was assigned to Hans Department. Hans, recognizing her talent, took her "under his wing" and has worked hard at mentoring her, bringing her in on discussions of special projects, and introducing her around the company.

Simona, at first, appreciated the doors that Hans was opening for her, but lately has seemed withdrawn and cold in her interactions with him.

Once Hans has assigned Simona to make an important presentation to a client. When time came for Simona to make presentation Hans went to the front of the room with her and, placing his hand on her shoulder for a moment, introduced her somewhat formally but glowingly as one of the shining lights of the Company. Simona looked visibly disturbed, and after her presentation left the meeting without speaking to her boss.

What do we recommend Hans Van der Strok, as a manager, in this situation?

9. Humor in Romania: from survival method during communism to ice-breaker in business

Romanians are by nature fun loving, warm, hospitable, playful, with an innate sense of humor, sometimes spiced with irony. Humor is a common part of the Romanian business culture.

Humor and jokes have the wonderful ability to invite us to think about what we don't like to think about even when the point is pleasant. That's why I think it's almost always worth the risk that we have the possibility of creating enough distance to break up laughing at the jokes.

Humor is part of the Romanian character, which includes even a fine appreciation of the absurd. It can be expressed spontaneously, at a different stage of business relationship. It is a tool to get to know people better, to establish better communication and to smooth the hardships in teams at work.

In Romania, humor was and still is very much appreciated. Some people say it was a way to survive through the communist past. It has been tied into the nation's value system, education and background. In a way, it is like children's lullabies: you need to grow up with them in order to appreciate them.

Humor serves different functions in different types of cultures. The more individualistic a culture, a group of people or an individual are, the more humor and jokes serve to gain attention. The reason being that people in most individualistic societies (these are all native English speaking countries) are good in presenting themselves, but generally bad in listening. That's why communication training—teaching "How to get my message across?'—is of utmost importance in these societies. That's why communication training tops the lists of management and leadership trainings there. That's why presentations, speeches, trainings by people raised in these countries often start with jokes and humor, in order to establish contact and to gain attention. Also after that, humor is interspersed whenever felt necessary to again raise attention

Less so in collectivistic cultures. Like in Romania. Humor and jokes may be used more cautiously, and introduced only once a satisfactory relationship has been established which is hoped to withstand the risk of misunderstandings.

For example, humor in Germany. An individualistic culture, but less strongly so than most other highly developed Western countries. Humor is used after a contact has been established and the work has been done. One wants first to be seen as a business person, to be taken seriously and only after, as a kind of reward and self-reward, "now we are allowed to move on to the lighter part" of the encounter. Jokes are also used to reduce tension or fill silence which itself is felt as creating tension (more than in England; this goes with the higher uncertainty avoidance in Germany).

Below is a joke I heard from one of my Romanian friends, who lived and worked in Germany for many years:

A foreign tourist in Germany asks for the way. The German broods on it, and then describes, „First, drive straight on, then you have to turn right at the third traffic light. You will pass a church. Achtung! It can easily be over-looked behind trees! 340 meters after the church the street will branch out. Follow the one half-left. Then you will cross—wait a minute—one, two, three, yes, three pedestrian crossings. Careful, don't count the pedestrian overcrossing in between. After the third pedestrian crossing drive on for six more blocks. Then you must veer right, sharp right, don't get confused with the other road turning right. Then, as soon as you see a tall building in the distance—the one at the left, not at the right!—you must get in the left lane! At the next crossing turn left, then again take the second right, and the street you are looking for will be the T-crossroad you are driving towards. It's easy to find!"

The foreigner responds wearily, "Thank you."

The German, „What do you mean 'thank you'? REPEAT!"

The Romanian friend who told me this joke also said: "I have worked with German colleagues for a long time. You are right when saying they have humor and when stressing the fact that they prefer starting with establishing a credible business relationship first. Humor is indeed something they share when feeling more confident with the other person and to reward a fruitful business relationship."

"It took me some time to realize this and I may have misused humor with these colleagues in the beginning. I very much like humor and tend to use it spontaneously when I feel comfortable. They kept some distance and made me feel "the outsider" until they could establish that business relationship they were looking for. After working together on a few projects, they finally accepted me as I was and we did have very nice moments. Ever since, humor has never been an obstacle... on the contrary," my friend also told me.

Let's try a fun, easy exercise:

If you think of Germans as coconuts and US Americans as peaches, what fruit would best be used to describe Romanians.

A. Kiwi—thin-skinned, but no big nut to crack.

B. Melons—you know where to cut in to find the sweet part.

C. Strawberries—nothing to peel, everything is accessible.

(A. Kiwi. The skin is the initial skepticism of Romanians at the start of your relationship. Once you are through that, and seen as friendly and reliable, there are practically no other big barriers.)

10. Romania through common stereotypes: vampires, Roma people, communism. What else?

For many foreigners, Romania is the equivalent of a series of common misconceptions. Things that just pop into one's mind when hearing about the country. We are talking about stereotypes and how they can affect communication. What was the first thing that came to your mind before you had the chance to discover the real Romania and its people?

Let's first clarify four of the most common stereotypes foreigners have about Romania. Some of them, such as the Roma information, may be hard to believe when thinking back at the recent European campaign against the Romanian-born Roma in France or Italy, for example. That certainly didn't help with clarifying the misconception!

1. There are no vampires in Transylvania. And there's nothing creepy about it and people living there don't have that funny accent you've heard in Hollywood films.

2. Romanians don't speak Russian, Romanian is a Romance language. People were forced to learn Russian during communism but this was not the case since 1990.

3. Roma people make up only 2.5% of Romania's over 22 million people. A surprising number of people seems to think Romanians are the minority. Which is not to say that Roma are not Romanians.

4. Bucharest is Romania's capital city, while Budapest is actually Hungary's. This is something that many people get wrong.

For more than forty years, Romanians lived under a regime that discouraged contact with foreigners. At a first meeting Romanians approach foreigners typically with the expectation that people from other cultures will take on their own (stereotypical) national identity. For example, on a scale, Canadians are supposed to be less aggressive than Americans, but not as direct as the French.

The ideological and legal barriers that once stood in Romania no longer exist and people are open to making contacts with foreigners. There are no taboo subjects, but foreigners will quickly note that people are more interested in talking about topics that touch their lives (such as personal, political, economic, or international situations) than talking about new subjects. Talking about work and asking where people come from are good ice-breakers, like talking about the weather.

My Canadian friend shared some of his experience in Romania. And I would like to share it with you:

"I found that discussion topics for Romanians that I met included where you are from, your family background (e.g. are you married, do you have children), what you are doing in Romania and what you think of Romania. On the latter point, I found that Romanians I spoke with were proud of their country, culture and history and would appreciate an honest but positive assessment of it.

When speaking with Romanians of European background I found touchy subjects to include the Roma people (so-called Gypsies). My experience was that European Romanians and the Roma have a difficult relationship. I often found that European Romanian friends and colleagues were aggressive and defensive towards any Roma who might approach me or other expatriates in their company.

Another potentially touchy subject for Romanians I came across was the Communist era. My experience was that younger Romanians want to move with certainty into a capitalist system and admired things "modern and Western"—albeit sometimes ambivalently. The older generation I found tended to recall the security of jobs and life that Communism offered.

While I often heard Romanians themselves sharply criticize Communism, I felt that this was a case of insider criticism being more acceptable than that of outsiders.

What leads to stereotyping?

Stereotypes are a more rigid form of generalization and contain an element of judgment in them. Stereotyping means fixing a set of ideas about what a particular nationality is like, which is (wrongly) believed to be true in all the cases:

- Chinese are hardworking/resilient
- Germans are well organized
- Italians are temperamental/passionate/touchy
- Latin people are lazy

- English are well mannered/have an excellent sense of humor
  - Americans are outgoing/friendly/materialistic
  - Swiss are trustworthy
  - French are hedonistic/amorous
  - people of color are musical
  - Arabs are excitable.

Stereotypes are usually based on exaggeration, distortion, ignorance, racism, cultural factors and historical experiences. Stereotyping is a negative, inadequate way of seeing people. Harmful stereotypes are retained unconsciously, are judgmental and not descriptive, could be accurate, but are often not and are not modified by experience.

Their aim is dividing, separating people between "them" and "us." They are a result of irritation because of our implicit values, those we cannot explain and we have learned unconsciously without ever questioning them, are being challenged. They do not consider individual and intracultural differences. They arise from the belief that culture is a barrier that we cannot overcome. They hide the intention of making the other culture accept my standards because they are better. In intercultural communication, cultural generalizations are used as a shorthand way to make non-judgmental cross-cultural comparisons, not to oversimplify or deny the complexity of social inter-action.

All people use stereotypes, but some people are more aware than others that the stereotypes they are used should be open to modification. Some people refuse to let stereotypes even when confronted with overwhelming evidence of challenges and undermines the stereotypes they hold. We have to ask ourselves why this is the case.

If we can understand what function or need negative stereotypes meet, then we can find a solution how to feel safer, easier, less frightened, more face saving. Then, perhaps, we can challenge negative stereotyping in ourselves, and others, more effectively.

Stereotypes can support basic feelings of self-esteem and even a need to feel superior. If you consider that you have grown up in a society that practices "proper" behavior, then you can look down on other cultures (or social classes within your own culture) that do not meet your "standards." Maybe your acceptance into one group is dependent upon your rejection of members of another group.

Generalizations are helpful to the extent that they are used only as guides, not as infallible recipes, or absolute truths. People's ethnic origin does not tell us exactly where they fit in terms of values or behaviors but it may alert us to possible areas of misunderstanding/miscommunication. Instead of relying on stereotypes, we should determine where each individual fits on a continuum of values, compared to his/her ethnic group.

We'd love to hear from you stories about situations when you found yourself using stereotypes about Romanians (or any other nation) and how the communication went. What other stereotypes have you heard about Romanians?

Alan Cornes' book "Culture from the Inside Out: Travel—And Meet Yourself," pages 39–45, can be very helpful developing the idea of stereotyping and generalization even further and connecting it to the Milton Bennett's Intercultural Developmental Model.

11. Intercultural intelligence: How the insiders play the game in Romania—organizational culture vs. national culture

In business and outside, Romania is a society of insiders. The basis of organizational life is the personal network. Newcomers without introductions or other personal credentials may find it difficult to break in. Organizational structure in traditional companies is strictly systematic and has hierarchical lines. Private companies have developed more streamlined processes and are prepared for the greater flexibility in changing volatile markets. Decision making is still concentrated at the top. What does it take to fit into these networks and processes in Romania?

Sabrina, the CEO of the Children-at-risk organization, who moved to Romania from the US recently, is a great picture of a leader who is very aware of culture's influence on the way she works. Despite the motivational challenges she faced with expanding into Romania, she showed me a list of questions she was trying to get answered to think about her strategy for this country. In addition, she talked about the differences between the programs her organization used in New York compared with those in Romania. Most of her board members are corporate executives so she presents the budget and strategic plan to them in an entirely different format from what she uses with her personnel and she uses yet another strategy with volunteers and donors.

Americans are used to informality, first names, humor, persistence, bluntness, technical competence, give-and-take bargaining and general consistency to what has been agreed. They wish to conclude the deal without unnecessary time wasting or labyrinthine procedures.

Romanians are known for different values due to a lot of invasion −prone territory which was expanding or contracting periodically: obsession to survive, volatility, unpredictability, tendency to blame others, social corruption, nepotism, self-importance, tendency to blame others. Personal contacts are highly recognized and very important to start any business activity. Business relationships remain formal. Frank and open discussion occurs at a later stage in a relationship. First names are for relatives and friends. In business, people use last names or professional titles when addressing each other. Socializing and hospitality during the day, in the evening or at weekends are an essential part of cementing the necessary personal relationships on which business relationships are based. Serious business may be done on these occasions away from protocol and formality of the office environment.

Sabrina represents a leader who sees the powerful role of Culture in how people think and behave.

*

Once, after a long day in the office, my friend Cristian took me to a football match in Bucharest. As we watched the game in the mixture of rain and sun, he started to explain the basic rules, the way scoring happened, and the ultimate goal of the game. Not only was the game starting to make sense but I actually felt myself getting drawn into the excitement of the competition. It would have been a sorry sight if I had actually tried to get out on the field and play. But at least I grew in my understanding of what was going on while the football professionals played their game.

Cultural knowledge provides a similar kind of understanding and perspective for the cultures with which we interact.
It involves understanding the rules, albeit often unspoken ones, that are behind the behavior occurring within a particular culture—among an ethnic group, within an organizational culture or within the subculture of a political party or religious group. The objective of the acquired understanding isn't to become like the people in that cultural group or to be able to play their games, but to understand and appreciate the rules behind their lives and society.

In the same way, culture consists of the rules and rationale behind the way life gets played in a particular context. The most familiar way of thinking about a cultural group is as a national culture (NC)—the norms, customs, and values shared with people who live in a country. For example, Romania has a national culture even though the country includes a variety of regions with 14 linguistic minorities, each with its own dialects and ethnic traditions.

The other culture most consistently encountered by leaders is organizational culture (OC). Organizations and even professions have their own distinct values, norms, and ways of viewing people and issues. Businesses have distinct ways of celebrating successes, motivating employees, and telling their stories. The same is true for universities, hospitals, and churches.

Which one has greater influence on employees' values, behavior, national culture (NC) or organizational culture (OC)?

The question is important because it leads us to investigate the degree of control that the headquarters of a multinational company can realistically exert on its subsidiary abroad, located in some other culture. If the OC has a stronger influence on values than the NC then management can directly determine the behavior of the subsidiary staff. If, on the other hand, NC has the stronger influence, then the HQ has to take the local values into account when imposing strategies, systems and structures; and how subsidiary staff interpret and implement these policies is strongly influenced by their NC.

As for the OC -every organization has its own culture and no two are the same, management builds the OC in order to analyze and to predict the attitude and behavior of the workforce in routine situations, members of the organization have to learn its culture.

The values of the NC are taught by family, friends, school, media, etc. The learning process is unconscious and is held at a deep level in the psyche.

Organizational values are learned much later and are assimilated at a more conscious level. The individual learns many of these OCs in maturity, and adopts an objective and critical attitude towards the learning.

Are organizational values so powerful? And influence the NC? It is important to know. Because if they ARE, employees can be conditioned to expressing values that contradict national values. In this case, HQ control over the OC of a foreign-based subsidiary is always insecure.

The evidence is ambiguous. There is no doubt that organizational values do influence the employees in the long term, and generate patterns of uniformity among organizational units, regardless of geographic, functional or business boundaries. But this does not mean that they operate as deeply as do the values of the NC, or significantly modify the NC when the two are in conflict. In practice, the influence on the individual may be determined less by management controls than by the length of time he/she stays in the organization.

The "job-hopper" who moves rapidly between companies, is unlikely to be much influenced by their cultures. On the other hand, the person who stays with one organization for all his/her career may be significantly affected. Small family companies can indeed impose this degree of control on members born within the organization.

*

Not everyone, however, is convinced about the relevance of cultural understanding. Roy, an American sales representative from a large manufacturing company, is a stocky forty-two-year-old man from the central part of the United States. When I talked to him, he was just a week away from making his second business trip to Romania to visit a couple of factories that were manufacturing his product line.

With his legs constantly moving up and down and his fingers nervously tapping on the table, he said, "Okay, no offense. But doesn't this whole cultural thing get a little overplayed? I mean, people are people and business is business. I'll probably have to eat some weird food next week, but otherwise, I don't see what the big differences are.

The way I see it, everyone is just trying to find a way to make a decent living and get ahead in life. I don't care whether you're Chinese, Mexican, or American, people are pretty much the same. They care about their kids like you and me. They know you have to be aggressive to survive in this global market. And everyone wants to make a decent living. The marketing strategy might need to adapt a little bit but I think manufacturing is manufacturing and selling is selling, wherever you go. Either you're cut out for it or not!"

Who, to your opinion, has a higher chance to establish an organizational culture in Romania, Roy or Sabrina?

The one who will take into consideration the National Culture!

12. Cultures doing business together: Romanians & Icelanders' communication pitfalls

A software company from Iceland offers a turn-key solution for gaming platforms and a large portfolio of games. It sold to a Romanian company a turn-key solution, a gaming platform as a base to be tailored to Romanians needs. Romanians believed it was the whole package including the turn-key solution, and this led to a series of misunderstandings. In this article we will analyze what might have caused the miscommunication between the Icelandic and the Romanian teams.

This misunderstanding has caused the Icelandic employees many additional unexpected hours of work and financial resources. The chief software architect says: "We are frustrated and feel that we have been taken advantage of and this is affecting the morale among the teams."

The Icelandic employees believe that the Romanians were purposely being ambiguous and vague during the negotiation process in order to obtain more work free of cost from the Icelanders.

Romanians believed, on the other hand, that the Icelanders were trying to mislead and made them buy the turn-key solution, making the Romanians think that everything was included in the sale (the platform including the work it takes to specifically construct it for the Romanian market).

The results of the data analysis showed that the misunderstanding between the Icelanders and the Romanian counterparts are multilayered, due to ***language barriers, different communication styles and other different business patterns and values.***

The Icelanders and Romanians generally communicate in English which was a native language for Icelandic workers and a foreign one for Romanians. The language barrier resulted in more frequent interaction among the Icelandic employees in the department and less between them and the Romanians, communicating across only very important issues, and then asking the best English speaker from the

Romanian team to be an interpreter. According to the Icelandic workers, the language barrier was a serious hurdle in their communication interaction, causing misunderstanding, mistakes and delays.

To understand this finding, it is important to know that English has become the primary foreign language taught in Romanian schools only recently. Many people over forty were not required to learn English as French was more common, so they learned English probably after they had left high school through private language schools or taking courses abroad.

According to the Icelandic Chief Software Architect, Romanians were vague on purpose about what they really wanted, while Icelanders wanted them to be more specific. Romanian people are less direct while Icelanders are more spontaneous. ***Romanian people generally consider direct confrontation inappropriate and impolite.***

The main difference between direct and indirect cultures shows that direct communication emphasizes low-context meaning and reveals the speaker's true feelings, opinions and needs, whereas indirect communication is a characteristic of a high-context culture and obscures or even disguises the speaker's true feeling, opinions and wishes.

Romanian workers preferred to reveal their opinions in private, not in front of a group. Or just wait and see what happens if they remain silent. Icelanders, on the other hand, are quite spontaneous and say directly what's on their mind. They rely very little on formal rules in their decision-making.

This may reflect the difference between Icelanders (a more individualistic culture) who use more self-oriented-saving strategies and Romanians (a more collectivist culture) who use more other-oriented strategies.

Another communication conflict reflected cultural differences in ***the pace of work and meeting deadlines.*** The Icelandic employees complained about projects taking too much time than originally planned. For example, writing a contract that they assumed would take about a month turned out to take five months. Meetings did not begin and end at the scheduled time and waiting for a response to an email message could take a week.

In terms of decision-making and planning, the Icelanders were not satisfied with Romanians who did not stick to previously-agreed decisions and kept ends open deliberately causing delays so they could make changes any time. Moreover, the Icelanders complained that the Romanians didn't seem to plan ahead of time, and if they did, the plan would probably change. The Icelanders were uncertain how to react in these kinds of situations as they did not want to appear too pushy.

Punctuality and timeliness (the importance or lack of importance placed on being "on time"), the use of time (how time is spent e.g. on completing a task or building relationship or conducting negotiations) showed more cultural differences.

It seems that the misunderstandings between Icelanders and Romanians are based on a combination of the first two elements. ***The Romanians perhaps do not place the same importance on punctuality and may prefer to spend more time in building relationships (which Icelanders see as less important than the task itself).***

According to the Icelandic employees, Romanians expected their managers have all the answers and tell them what to do and how. This situation occurs in a very formal hierarchical structure that can take a very long time resulting in delays and deadlines being missed because of too much attention being paid to details.

On the other hand, superiors in Iceland are less autocratic than the Romanian ones and the differences between the bosses and subordinates are not clearly marked. Because the hierarchy in Iceland is relatively flat, the communication between the managers and the subordinates is faster and issues are managed more rapidly.

Icelanders belong to a low power distance culture where they believe that less hierarchy is better and that power should only be used for legitimate reasons. In contrast, ***Romania belongs to a high power distance culture where the hierarchy is valued and there is a wider gap between superiors and subordinates with more formal relationship between them.***

This miscommunication between the Icelanders and the Romanians is still unresolved and the Icelanders are currently working on the platform in Romania, mostly for free.

Mergers and acquisitions that take place more and more nowadays within national borders are challenged and may result in frustration, resistance, and conflicts for employees and management, cultural differences in communication style and work-related values seem to put some pitfalls on the way to successful results.

Have you ever been in a situation like this?

13. Doing business à la grecque in Romania; an intercultural perspective

Greek investments have a long history in Romania with Greece being among the first countries to invest in Romania after the revolution in 1989. Romania has always been attractive to the Greeks since both countries share very strong historical, social and cultural ties and businessmen of Greek origin have been living and thriving in Romania for centuries. The geographical proximity of the two countries and the size of Romania's potential is one of the basic reasons for the Greek business here. Let's look at the way Greeks and Romanians communicate and act in business.

The main sectors in which Greek businesspeople invested in Romania are telecommunications, banks, insurance, real estate, food industry and commerce. Greek investors were sure that the country's heavy economic crisis in 2008-2009 would not affect the companies present in Romania and thus the Romanian economy would not to be threatened by the evolutions in Greece. After the economic measures taken by the Greek and Romanian governments, the commercial exchanges between the two countries are expected to increase, offering new perspectives for the region. With nearly 5,000 companies registered here in 2011 and employing some 22,000 people, Greek investors have so far pumped around EUR 4 billion into the Romanian economy. Briefly, this is the recent statistics about Greek business in Romania. But... What do we know about Greek business partners? And what are the touching points for Romanian business people?

The Greek view of leadership is similar to the French concept—that is, **rooted in rational argument and skill in oratory.** Mastery of the language is seen as essential for commanding the respect of subordinates. Traditional leadership style is **quite directive.** Greeks work best in teams with **a strong leader,** who ultimately takes all the decisions and is then careful to make sure they are carried out. Individual leadership coexists with the team work. This combination of extreme **individualism and collec-**

tivism can be confusing to Romanian people. It can be very productive in a small and paternalistic environment that Romanian people are used to, but frequently leads to factionalism in larger organizations.

The meeting is a forum for the dynamic expression of strong personal opinions, preferable contrary to everyone else. Each person will be listened and energetically argued with. This situation looks scary to Romanian employees who avoid directly conflicting arguments and contradictions. Formal meetings are arranged only for very important issues. Frequent informal coordination and briefing meetings are more common. There is seldom a formal agenda and rarely are there formal minute. The quality of cooperation and communication depends largely on the personal relationships.

Forecasts and plans are the preserve of the senior management and remain subject to constant amendment. The plan is a tool for negotiating with banks and shareholders rather than a management device.

Status is important for both partners—Greek and Romanian and can be gained in different ways. There is great respect ***for education, qualifications and intellectual prowess*** on the one hand, ***wealth and connections*** on the other hand. The major consideration for preferment is whether the person can be trusted rather than his qualifications, expertise or performance. This is the basis of the nepotism, political affiliation and personal influence—similar in both countries.

Trust is the basis on which outsiders are also judged. They are genuinely welcomed as a source of new ideas and expertise, international contacts and influence, but any suspicion that they are exploiting the relationship or attempting to dominate will be detrimental. Trust is the key element in relationships in Romania, or the lack of it.

Greece is a tactile culture. Its distance of comfort is similar to the Italian one, and hugging and kissing are common. ***Greeks are usually late for appointments,*** but they always have a good excuse and warm apologies.

Greeks often ***display great charm,*** but they are ***serious negotiators*** and know their business well. The senior person will dominate the discussion, as this is the rule in the Mediterranean countries. They are shrewd, have great experience and do not give much away. Something for Romanian business people to learn.

Greeks are ***skilled debaters*** and employ a whole gamut of verbal and physical expressions. To

Romanian outsiders, used to a more restrained mode of expression, what appears like a full-blown argument may be a quite innocuous exchange of views.

Personal contact is important. Only when it is impossible to meet face to face the telephone will be used. There is a distrust of written communication. ***Humor is frequently enjoyed in business*** as anywhere else. It is witty, satirical, and pointed, especially where government is concerned. Looks like the reason why Greeks are in Romania!

In a traditional company the titles and positions are irrelevant. There is one boss who takes all the responsibility. He is the owner or has the owner's trust. Below him is a narrow and vertically oriented hierarchy of subordinates who are delegated specific tasks and have little responsibility. This approach works better in a small and medium-sized family companies than in a large or state-owned organizations. Corporate structure of the big companies has a board of at least three directors elected by shareholders. The chief executive is either a general manager or a managing director.

Compared with Romania there is little discrimination against women. They are well represented in the professions and in politics and their opportunities in business, like those for men, depend more on their connections than their gender.

Despite a tradition of political and economic crisis, for a country with such an ancient and revered past, Greece has a propensity for constantly remaking itself. The latest transformation over the past few decades is from an underdeveloped Balkan backwater on the fringes of Europe to a modern mixed economy as part of the EU.

As you can see, Romania's business partner and neighbor—Greece—is similar and quite different in many ways. Which way will prevail and lead the business here in future? How much local companies with Greek investments will be influenced by these differences and crisis traditions? Or how much similarities will tighten the business partnerships between Romania and Greece?

14. From Russia with love. Russians (and Romanians) doing business

Culturally speaking, everything is in place for good business and commercial communication between Russia and Romania. But despite some high profile interests, Russia lies outside the top ten investors to Romania in the official national statistics. Russia has been close enough to Romania and has had an influence on Romania long enough to lend it some of the main traits in doing business. Here we'll look at how Russians do business. What do we have in common and where do we accomplish each other in business?

A Moscow-based IT company has opened an office in Romania, which is the first country in the EU where the company has established its presence. The strategy of the company on a new market is a software license reselling as a footprint. Target clients—small businesses which represent 95% of the total number of companies. Further steps in adding business segments are consultancy, IT auditing, outsourcing and education.

Long-term plans. How will the company accomplish them?

In order to answer this question and give some advice to this company lets analyze three main areas:

1. Russian style of doing business
2. Genesis of Russian leadership style
3. Stages of the Russian business history

How do Russians do business?

In business, Russians play chess: they plan several moves ahead. They often present an initial draft to a business partner outlining all the objectives. But this is only a starting point. Their approach to an agreement is conceptual and all-embracing. Contracts are not as binding in the Russian mind as in Western minds. They see it binding only if the contract continues to be mutually beneficial. Anything introduced as an official directive or regulation will be distrusted. What is indicated as a personal recommendation will be embraced. Russians are basically conservative and do not accept change easily. In business they often push and understand being pushed, but they rebel if they feel the pressure is intolerable. They achieve what they do largely through an intricate network of personal relationships. Favor is repaid by favor. They enter meetings unsmiling, but they can be quickly melted with a show of understanding and sincerity.

Russians are people-oriented rather than deal – oriented. Bear in mind during business relationship that their priorities are personal relationships, form and appearance, and opportunities for financial gain—in that order. Russians are not smiling, but essentially warm, emotional, caring people, eagerly responding to kindness and love. In order to build strong relationship with Russian people one should indicate his human side. They are sensitive and proud and status conscious and must be treated as equals.

Though there is no long-term alternative to the EU Russia's "Europeanness" many characteristics are mirrored in Western Europe: compassion in Italy, sentimentality in Germany, love of tradition in Britain, warmth and generosity in Spain, artistic achievements in France. Plus other positive traits: stamina, powers of improvisation, deep friendships.

Genesis of Russian leadership style

Modern societal culture in Russia is determined by traditional features, historically developed through centuries, by the influence of 20th century totalitarianism and by the radical revolution in values, beliefs, and behaviors through the transitional 1990s and early 2000s.

Historically developed characteristics of Russian culture are rooted in Slavic history, Orthodox religion, and specific features of the natural environment. Through the centuries, Russia has integrated basic values of both the West and the East—reason and inspiration. It has served as a bridge between Western and Eastern cultural traditions with a certain psychological dependence on both. Its national character combined such qualities as habitual, patient struggle with misfortune and hardship; the ability to concentrate efforts; the ability to cooperate across a large geographic distance, impersonal collectivism; humanism; and the search for truth.

While Russia was growing through the centuries, its leaders were traditionally associated with the state, religion, or the military. Peter the Great, who began

"Westernization" in the 18th century by autocratic and barbarian means, was an admired military leader. Business leaders in his time were traders who, along with the military, created Europe's strongest military industrial complex of the time. Later, the economic liberalism of Catherine the Great attracted the highest-ranking Russian nobles to entrepreneurship. The industrial revolution in the 19th century brought the real spirit of private initiative and leadership to Russia. Talented business leaders such as Morozov, Knopp, and Ryabushinski founded successful business empires in Russia and introduced many organizational innovations, including charitable initiatives.

In the 20th century, under Socialism, in contrast to the West, Russia appeared to have largely retained, even in periods of rapid industrial expansion, an autocratic or patrimonial system (single-centered).

Russian leadership characteristics were modified by specific Soviet (totalitarian) traits such as a perception of the environment as hostile and dangerous, supremacy of society's goals over the individual's, and a relativistic view of morality with an acceptance of double standards in life

In the 1990s, the transitional Russian economy was run by a small number of financial industrial groups, arguably more powerful than the state. The stage of aggregating capital by selling state property ("privatization stage") was over, and the new epoch could be defined as the stage of "managing capital effectively," with the oligarchs—leaders of industrial and financial empires—displaying a new leadership model for the Russian economy.

The heterogeneous kaleidoscopic culture of Russia's current transitional society is different from the homogenous Soviet culture. Business leaders and managers in Russia are motivated by one or a combination of the following business philosophies:

– bureaucratic, based on active initiatives under state-run bureaucratic supervision;

– pragmatic, based on maximum profitability on a technocratic basis;

– predatory, based on achieving success through tough suppression of rivals including Mafia connections, growth by any means, and cheating on partners, consumers, and the state; and

– socially responsible, based on linking business to the promotion of national interests, the resolution of social problems, and universal human values.

Root characteristics of the stages of Russian business history

The first group, the Old Guard, consists of those who proved their talents as leaders in large-scale projects such as managing technological innovations. The Old Guard exploits their access to key decision-making centers and information and use bureaucratic connections and control of resources. These people still keep leading positions in large industrial corporations or in internationally competitive sectors of the economy (oil-and-gas, aerospace, shipbuilding, and others).

The second group, the New Wave, emerging from economic reforms, follows a different road to economic independence by searching for innovations and reflecting advanced economic thinking. They are leaders of the former shadow economy, which has been increasingly legalized and are former Communist party functionaries or military officers who successfully transformed into businessmen. A large proportion of this group is young people, hungry for entrepreneurial success.

The third group of people, who can be called Forced Entrepreneurs, are forced to take initiatives due to fear of unemployment and are now involved primarily in small-scale trade transactions.

Finally, there is a group of foreign businessmen (International Corps) that operates in the Russian market, including representatives of the Russian Diaspora.

The IT company has been active on the Romanian market for 10 years followed by some other software and IT companies. What do you think were the reasons?

Steel and aluminum products is another field which companies from Russia found attractive and built their production lines in Romania.

15. Virtual multicultural teams: real communication in the virtual world

The following situation sounds common enough for Romania, a country which has been chosen by many companies as their outsource location. The cheaper and more skilled labor force, plus the expansion of online technologies make it easy for Romanians to telework with colleagues in other countries. But how easy is it to communicate with them?

Let's start with the following situation:

"A company based in the United States develops multimedia software with a team of 7 free-lance developers located in 3 different countries, including Romania. The team was formed through Internet chat groups or interpersonal relations and is completely virtual. All developers are under commercial contract with the main company. The company has no offices and developers have never met with each other. All employees telework from home and informally communicate through electronic means. Each developer has specific tasks and is in charge of one part of the software development. They plan the work together at the beginning of each project. They work on the same data file and post their contributions on a collaborative platform. The company's job is to assemble the different pieces developed by the teleworkers."

Many companies use virtual teams of geographically dispersed people to work on short—and long-term projects. A long-term "virtual" team is one that conducts its work almost entirely through electronic technology. Such technology and the expansion of global business have changed the work environment for organizations of all sizes, allowing even small companies to compete in the international market place. Communicating across cultures using technology can be a difficult task. It requires understanding the advantages and limitations of technology and how to build relationships via technology.

Though it gives an opportunity for frequent, easy, low-cost, around-the-clock communion and collaboration, virtual team members need to choose an appropriate communication channel for their purposes and be sure to balance distance work with face-to-face communication. Learning how to handle the technology and to deal with different cultures poses the biggest challenges.

How do you supervise team members you don't see? Results, rather than time and effort, are what you do see. Therefore, outputs become primary. In many cases virtual projects create a 24-hour workday distributed around the world. Here work and time management styles that differ culturally and personally, and work on building trust around the difference should be discussed. And health and safety implications of virtual work, not just use of technology, but its psychology, the stress it creates and its impact on the lifestyle of the workers should be examined.

Virtual culture clashes with organizational culture

Remember that organizational culture is, most of the time, a particular expression of regional and ethnic culture. The values and behaviors of virtual project management can seem threatening if they are not already a part of the culture of the larger organization. They need to be fully communicated, understood, wrestled with and accepted if the organization is to support the implementation of virtual project management and realize the benefits that it offers.

Hard feelings may arise, for example, if the virtual team operates with "flat" values in a hierarchical organization, like in Romania. Suspicion and resentment may surface if "work" is defined in terms of hours spent in an office and virtual workers may not be found there on the normal schedule.

Another typical feature for Romania in organizational cultures where information is highly guarded, used as power or traded as currency, virtual teamwork and the corporate intelligence it creates will be affected. Expectations may be frustrated and little value added may result from virtualizing business operations in such environments. Therefore successful implementation of virtual working may require that we work out agreements about sharing people's time information in ways that fit, as well as challenge the existing culture; and reward sharing psychologically and reinforce it by the compensation system. People should start to think automatically, "You are not a real professional unless you share effectively."

At the same time, take security concerns most seriously and work out the needed protocols and commitments to prevent leaks and invasions that could subvert the project.

Relationships of individuals and project teams working virtually

The members of the virtual project teams will need to become culturally competent, at least in respect to their own members, if they are to manage diversity issues. There are **some diversity advantages** to virtual working, however. Skin color, gender and other biases based on visual factors will be minimized when the group works in technology that is limited to audio and written transmission. Individuals who by ethnicity or personality are less outspoken in face-to-face situations may contribute more to newsgroups and forums that provide more offline time to prepare a response, or where they enjoy anonymity or less exposure.

Finally, face-to-face meetings, when they do happen, can be made to be of a higher quality. They can be used to focus mainly on the important issues of vision, planning and above all, motivation and teambuilding and culture management rather than lower level data sharing and technical discussion that can be done by virtual means prior to and as a follow-up to the face-to-face sessions.

Mismatch of cultural context in virtual communication

In individualistic cultures (Northern Europe, North America) commonly the MESSAGE is all that is needed for the recipient to respond or take action. A person from such an individualistic culture may send a one-line e-mail request, but to act or respond a person from a more collective culture (in varying degrees—Southern US, Eastern Europe, Asia, Latin America) may need to know: Who (status, role) is the sender? Why was this message written? Who else in my organization knows about this or needs to know about it? What information, consensus or permission do I need from others in order to respond?

How can this be addressed? Training can help to understand the importance and nature of differing contexts on both sides. Use face-to-face time to get project teams started in this direction and to maintain them. Encourage virtual workers and teams to build common context for teamwork by providing personal information, pictures, accomplishments, titles, roles in the system. Allow for online time for introductions, warm-ups, and chitchat about things especially people you have in common. Encourage social events and personal forums online.

Individualistic cultures stress what you can do and what you know. Despite similar technical capabilities, more collective cultures (like in Romania) often stress who you are and whom you know. In one case, facts, data, and deadlines get things done; in the other, relationships, contacts, and roles get things done.

Inappropriate, unprepared, incorrect, or blunt responses from the "what" cultures cause loss of face in the "who" cultures for: the sender, the sender's superior and subordinates as well as for the recipient and his or her network.

The use of time

In individualistic cultures, time is money. In collective person oriented cultures, relationship is money (and much more). This often results in mismatch of expectations around use of time, response time, meeting deadlines that may not be sorted out as easily in virtual environments as they are face to face.

When polychronic (human multitasking) cultures face monochronic (one-thing-at-a-time) cultures each sees the other as respectively narrow-minded or distracted. Polychronic individuals may seem less committed to the team or differ in how they arrange work because they have multiple responsibilities. Different uses of time may not be immediately apparent in virtual working because they are less visible and often masked by time-zone differences.

Cultural preferences for certain technologies

Cultures may prefer or resist the use of certain media or technologies at different times and in different contexts. For example, where saving face is important, there may be embarrassment about such simple things as one's spelling skills when contributing to forums or e-mail, and concern about giving unprepared, quick, imperfect answers in real time connections.

Some individuals and groups may resist certain technologies because they reinforce a power imbalance between first and second language speakers or writers, such as native English speakers and English as the Second language speakers. Second language speakers become an out-group.

Eliminating cultural differences is practically out of question. **Most global players do not consider intercultural diversity as an obstacle; on the**

contrary, they perceive it as an asset. In the market understanding, it creates an appreciable competitive advantage.

What is your experience of virtual multicultural teams? What is your experience with the Romanians who are part of these teams?

16. Motivation across cultures: what drives Romanians to work?

Motivating all level employees to use their brains and not their backs and strive on behalf of an organization is a difficult task, and when it comes to a diverse set of people from different cultures it is even more difficult. What drives Romanians to work and what motivates employees with a different cultural background?

Let's take the example of a mix Romania-Dutch project. Since 2005, the Province of Overijssel (Netherlands) has been cooperating with Teleorman County—located in the South of Romania—in the field of water management, initially on drinking water and wastewater. However, after Teleorman County was hit by three severe floods in 2005, Overijssel decided to initiate the "Teleorman Flood Risk Management Pilot Project" (October 2006—June 2009). The project was carried out by a team consisting of a mix of seven Romanian and Dutch organizations.

The organizational structure and flood risk management are not the subject of our analysis. But the motivation across cultures was something that attracted our attention as water projects are "processes of social interaction" in which various actors from different cultures jointly solve a complex unstructured problem.

In this particular case the cooperation between various project participants developed positively. Even though some of the Romanians were skeptic in the beginning, they were all positive about the project results. Their reason to participate in the project was gaining access to Dutch expertise and money. The Dutch wanted to participate on economic and social responsibility reasons. Conflicts of interests never emerged during this project.

The Romanians and Dutch were mutually dependent: Dutch organizations provided financial resources as well as management models and construction methods, while Romanian partners arranged all necessary permits and licenses.

In addition to the partners' own objectives, external pressure and self-effectiveness assessment—"social relations" may also be regarded as a source of motivation. The development of relations and trust, joint institutional learning influenced the application of Dutch expertise. More broadly speaking, collective learning process was crucial in solving water problems. As a result—the Dutch-Romanian cooperation in flood risk mapping "could be extended to other flood prone areas in Romania."

According to the project leader, project participants were extremely motivated to participate. Even though the project was initiated and designed in the Netherlands, everybody was enthusiastic from the beginning. The project leader said that the level of motivation was not negatively affected by various project delays, which had financial or economic nature. He did not observe any conflict of interests; everybody was like-minded. Interviews with Romanian participants confirmed this good cooperation. Why would Dutch people come and tell them what to do? And, why would Dutch approaches be useful to reduce flood risks in Romania? This skepticism disappeared during the project. Both parties discovered that the Dutch and Romanian approach to flood risk management was quite similar. Furthermore, many meetings were organized in which both Dutch and Romanian experts were involved. During these meetings Dutch experts really listened and were always willing to adapt their existing ideas. This collaboration (in particular with the project leader), was often informal and based on friendship and supported by highly motivated people on both Dutch and Romanian side. They still keep contacts with the leader asking for advices and other support. They also added that he was always able to come with a clear list of priorities. The added value of the cooperation for Romanians is that it makes the impossible possible, such as innovative designs. By supporting such activities with money, the Dutch partner proved that he was really committed to those idea. Project selection was based on expert judgment and did not involve political preferences.

Working with a global workforce is clearly not an easy task. Even so, the task can be made somewhat easier if managers have a frame or a tool box that can provide some structure for observation, understanding and action. In our case we tried to examine the challenges of working with employees from different cultures through the lens of work motivation. In doing so, we can raise three questions:

Firstly, on a general level, what is it that motivates (or fails to motivate) employees on the job?

Secondly, on a more specific level, do these motivational drivers differ across cultures?

And **thirdly,** what is the role played by managerial efforts to involve employees in work related discussions in securing employee motivation and performance?

All these questions relate to the use of Human Capital and maximization of return on their human resources.

Differences in employee behavior can be found all over the world.

British and Canadian companies motivate their employees primarily through financial incentives, while Dutch companies focus on providing employment stability and employee benefits. Indonesian and Korean companies prefer rigid and often autocratic organizational hierarchies where everyone knows their place, while Swedish and Norwegian companies stress informality, power sharing and mutual benefit in the workplace. Some countries, like Germany, even combine them all.

Managers should recognize this critical behavior and the influence it puts on the company's performance.

Work motivation is defined as that which energizes, directs, and sustains human behavior in the workplace. Without highly motivated workforce that uses its brains, and not just its backs, competitive advantage becomes highly problematic. Simply put, competitive organizations need all of their employees striving on behalf of the organization's goals and objectives, not just the people at the top. The challenge for the global manager is to accomplish this within a work context where behavior is often determined by cultural variations beyond their control.

Cultural drivers can create both the opportunities and constraints on efforts by managers and organizations to motivate their employees through various incentive and reward systems.

Ex. Culture 1: Manager's normative beliefs about social relationships and time/work patterns (belief in individualism, monochronic behavior) => Culturally compatible approach to motivation (preference for goals and targets, performance-based compensation) => Manager's approach to work motivation (use of management-by-objectives programs, merit-based compensation tied to individual performance) <=>

Culture 2: Employees' normative beliefs about social relationships and time/work patterns (belief in collectivism, polychronic or multitasking behavior) => Culturally compatible approach to motivation (preference for general goals and targets, seniority or group-based compensation) => Employee response

(lack of employee buy-in or commitment, resistance to intra-group competition, poor work attitudes)

Cultural drivers influence both managerial and employee strategies and preparedness for motivation. Sometimes in opposite directions. Each side has predispositions concerning what constitutes a fair day's work and a fair day's pay. Presumably, where both sides agree this to be fair, employee effort and performance would be expected to increase as might mutual trust and commitment. Where perceptions of unfairness emerge or remain, however, motivational expectations or employee motivations would likely decline. In this equation it is important to remember that both managers and employees can have very different perceptions of what fairness means and, to some extent, this is influenced by cultures and experience.

Fortunately this example could not be applied to our case!

In your experience, what motivates Romanians to work?

17. Explicit, implicit communication and the Barbarian reflex. Where do Romanians fit?

Everything you do—conveys a message, on different layers. These layers can be either the High Context—meaning that you communicate not only with words, but with voice, tone, body language and so on, or Low Context, which goes to say you expect explicit communications. Some cultures fall in the first categories, others, in the second. Where do Romanians fit in?

Romanians are oratorical by nature and are proud of their sophistication in discourse. They rarely answer questions with "yes" or "no." It is better to hint at what you want and then be prepared to read between the lines. Their answers are in any case long and complex and may to some extent reflect what you want to hear. Their delicacy is Italian in nature, as is their capacity for flexible truth when questioned aggressively. So **Romanians are related to the high-context culture.**

We should delve a bit into that. **High Context cultures** (France, Italy, Spain, Mexico, Greece, Arab countries, East European countries, Japan, China, Korea) communicate meaning not only with words, but with voice, tone, body language, facial expressions, eye contact, speech patterns, and the use of silence. Words play a relatively small part in the overall meaning of the communication, and the context conveys the bulk of the information. People in high-context cultures, such as Asia and South America, tend to take time getting to know one another, providing for an understanding of the broader context of a conversation. This results in knowledge of what to expect, what signals to look for, and how to interpret subtle signs or expressions—fewer words need to be said.

What else about Romanians, from this perspective? They are attentive but suspicious listeners, who may interrupt you if anything you say seems contradictory. They are used to lengthy presentations and arguments, so if you are too brief you will not make much impact. It is important to establish parameters at the outset of any business discussion, fixing procedures, limits and ultimate positions.

Romanians will not be deterred from attempting to gain advantage, but once they have understood your position, they can behave in a constructive, creative and charming manner.

At meetings, extensive small talk is a necessary preamble. When the Romanians get down to business their statements must be taken with a pinch of salt. If you disagree with them, show this obliquely, as they hate being snubbed in any way.

On the other hand, **Low Context cultures** (Germany, Scandinavian countries, US, Canada) are expecting explicit communications. People want detailed background information before making a decision; however they are generally unaware of subtle nonverbal signals going on around them. Documents and contracts are not taken seriously unless written or signed—details must be provided. For example, in the United States and Germany (both low-context cultures), contracts with numerous explicit clauses are a normal way to conduct business and the written word is taken quite literally. In low-context cultures, expect detailed documentation—thorough job descriptions, detailed accounting, and lengthy business planning documents. The devil is in the detail.

Leveraging high-context and low-context cultures means relying on both implicit and explicit communication—carefully ensuring that what you say (low-context) is always mirrored by what you do (high-context).

Switching to the "Barbarian-reflex" while communicating

Higher context cultures are more common in the eastern cultures than in western, and in countries with low racial diversity. A lower context culture tends to explain things further, and it is thought that this may be related to the need to accommodate individuals with a wide variety of backgrounds.

When communications become challenging, it can be tempting to access your "barbarian-reflex", especially when messaging becomes unclear. We should focus a bit on that. Both the ancient Romans and Greeks called all foreigners "Barbarians." The word "barbarian" refers to the uncultured or to those with unrefined communication skills—both explicit and implicit. The way we express ourselves is pre-determined by our differing cultures (even if we often do speak the same language). How we communicate ultimately determines how we are viewed as global leaders.

As you can imagine, it is completely ineffective to view your colleagues, staff, or even clients as "foreign" or "unrefined" simply because they do not communicate as you do. If you are motivated to communicate effectively on a multicultural level, you will need to invest in building trust—the more you come to know someone, the less you tend to look upon him or her as a "barbarian."

If your purpose is to ensure your colleagues and staff reliably implement to your specifications, the strategy you choose will vary depending on the cultural orientations you are working across. In those high-context cultures, your strategy will need to be relationship and trust based and may not be explicit—more soft-skills based and time intensive. In low-context cultures the purpose of communication is to transfer information and your strategy will need to be explicit, efficient, and detailed in order to ensure the correct implementation.

Damaging miscommunications can (and do) happen frequently when working across cultures, but they can be avoided if we apply some cultural intelligence to our diverse interactions—in particular, understanding the differences between high and low context communications and leveraging both for personal and organizational gain.

18. Management culture in Romania: what does the boss say?

Romania, now a member of the EU, has for so many years been a society where management authority was highly concentrated in the hands of a few people who could wield their authority in quite an arbitrary way. The management style was often autocratic and the main expectation of the workforce was that of quiet obedience. But then came foreign managers and things started to change.

The nature of management varies between societies and dominant cultural norms shape the style of management in different countries. It is not enough for the Western businessman to "think global, act local." It is also important that they **think about** the local and **know something about it.**

A manager-owner of the company called "Beta" demands complete obedience from his employees and imposes himself as a model. The words repeated daily are "You are here to shut up, listen and learn" and "the intelligent employee is the one who knows how to imitate his manager." His own model is an English manager under whom he worked in Indonesia for a number of years in the 1990's and who (as he asserts) even checked the cleanliness of their nails and hair as part of the daily control. Though he would not go so far, our manager would require a certain make-up, a certain lipstick color, a certain length of hair and skirts from his employees who are all university students or graduates aged 20 years or more. The boss is always right and making him try to recognize his mistakes always ends up in threats and scandals. The counterpart is that the manager provides indeed his employees with useful practical courses of marketing strategy, taught with passion and certain professionalism. His tactics is to alternate coercion with paternalism (the stick and the carrot). His main piece of advice is "do not trust anybody in business." For this manager both the workplace and the business world are competitive places, thus, the rule of mistrust should be applied both within and outside the enterprise. Employees have no right to have their own ideas and depend on him for the smallest decision, under the threat of being fired. Despite the lack of real power of the intermediary managers in the organization, hierarchy is very much emphasized by the manager. This is meant to impress potential employees invited to collective interviews and potential clients invited to buy a product. "Impressing" the client by word and gesture is a recurrent theme in the discourse of the manager.

Another example.—The management of the NGO "Alpha" is situated at the opposite extreme, their manager trying to maintain a democratic regime, in which highly educated employees are encouraged to participate in management decisions. Every single employee is paid attention to and consulted before s/he is allocated an activity and monthly democratic meetings are organized for planning the activities of the enterprise. These meetings last forever and often do not lead to concrete results, because their goal is to reach an unanimous agreement and this is difficult, even where there are only ten employees. And though democratic voting could be used, the meeting is practically postponed until the manager privately persuades each employee of the qualities of the decision of the majority.

Here I would like to pay your attention to the finance sector in Romania as one of the most dynamic sectors of Romanian economy. Its banking segment is overwhelmingly based on foreign European capital (Greece, Austria, the Netherlands, Italy, Hungary, France, Portugal, etc.). Consequently, a significant part of the top management in the Romanian foreign owned banks came from Europe, and/or has had training and experience in Western leadership and management styles. They saw themselves as exemplars of the new management agenda (ex.: strategic approach, less authority, team working, flexibility, participation). Some were modeling the behavior of lower level managers (ex: networking, motivational leadership, transparency, trust building, etc.).

For older senior staff "cultural change" often meant a process of denying the values of a lifetime and painfully acquiring the skills of the new age. For younger managers it was a new road to liberalization.

Almost all organizations experienced "cultural blocks" or "resistances" to the participative, pro-active and empowered management which the Anglo-American model of management implied to societal culture and history as the key explanatory variables.

This management culture values things like overcoming status barriers between grades and levels; experimenting with new "consulting" styles in facilitating teams of "knowledge workers"; building flexible communication systems; empowering staff with more authority.

What did Romanians make of all these?

Senior managers attributed this expectation of higher direction to a fear of making mistakes and being punished. Middle and lower level Romanian managers seemed to lack confidence in their own judgment and preferred to follow instructions rather than solve problems. Equally, managers could seem reluctant to take initiative or to stand out and be held personally accountable for a line of action. Some managers appeared to hide behind procedures, evade responsibility and avoid risk.

Under the old order management authority in Romania had been highly concentrated in the hands of a few people who could wield their authority in quite an arbitrary way, without the checks and balances you would expect in the West. The management style was often autocratic and the main expectation of the workforce was that of quiet obedience.

Romanian managers typically liked to brief their direct line subordinates on a one– to—one basis, to give prescriptive instructions and to follow up on an individual basis to see that action had happened.

Participation was something new in Romania. Reserve and suspicion seemed to cast a long shadow and were not easily banished. Romanian managers in a team are often wary of each other. Especially at the beginning of relationships it was difficult to get full and open discussion. Team dynamics often seemed to involve protecting your position and skillfully maneuvering around people.

Historically, in the atmosphere of fear and uncertainty introduced by Communism, information was a commodity to be stored and traded in Romania, a source of status and power.

Traditionally, trust was limited in Romanian organizations. The top has not shown trust in lower levels performing their work without close scrutiny and lower levels have not trusted top managers to think beyond their own interests.

However, co-existing with this mistrust there may also be an implicit social contract between higher and lower levels. Lower managers and workers have traditionally accepted hierarchical chains of status, tough authoritarian control and downward communication in return for protection, the security of clear direction and the manager as the "good father figure."

Like the boyars during old times, many older Romanian managers seemed to believe that they had a duty to lead and also to protect. This may also explain the continuing paternalism of much Romanian management. At a time of global pressures to restructure organizations and keep large numbers of workers, managers in Romania have often tried to preserve jobs and provide a measure of social protection.

A typology of Romanian managers

Here is management culture in the form of a "typology" of management orientations to be found today in Romania:

a) Traditional Managers: These are largely unreformed managers who behave according to the administrative rules of hierarchy, procedure, bureaucracy and process. These may be largely found in the state managed enterprises. These can appear like "yesterday's manager."

b) Entrepreneurial managers: These are managers who are committed to entrepreneurial activity. They are leading new start enterprises or engaged in innovation and restructuring in more established companies to achieve economic success. They have flexible, market-led attitudes. Some will be from the old order who were able to transfer their skills of "playing the system" under communism to new conditions, others will come from a new class of young owner/entrepreneurs or managers.

c) Paternalist managers: These are the managers who are attempting to introduce change so that their enterprises become more effective in market terms yet are still led by social values ex.: recognizing communal obligations; maintaining employment where they can; addressing social and human issues. This group could act as a block to developing economic change. Or can become a new kind of manager—the participative innovating reformer.

d) Missionary managers: These are the expat managers from the West investing in Romania because of its low cost base and good technical skills, who are often the protagonists for a new management culture. They can be part of the solution if they act as agents for knowledge transfer, facilitators of experimentation and exemplars for modernization. However, they can also be part of the problem if they expect foreign techniques work equally well in Bucharest without interpretation and adaptation.

e) Self seeking managers: These are the managers who recognize the new opportunities in a transition economy which gives special opportunities to insiders to enrich themselves through privatization and favored business relationships, etc. These are the "nomenklatura managers" who know how to use their networks to make short term gains. They are also the "nouveau riches" and crime linked businessmen who can use the new uncertainties for their own advantage.

Management transition

Management culture in Romania is in a period of transition. There is a Romanian saying: "Brains take a long time to melt after a hard winter." The brains of Romanian managers are still opening to the possibilities of new ways of managing. Management culture is shifting from the homogeneity of communism to the heterogeneity of the market. Shadows of the old "Stalinist" management, of autocratic paternalism, of centralism and "scientific management" in the workplace still delay. But the new economy is creating new social groupings whose interests are tied to economic success through the market. Organizations are adapting to the demands of external forces like EU in order to survive. Multinational companies are acting as vehicles for new technology, knowledge and management practice. Romanian managers themselves are recognizing that old rules no longer apply and are reaching for new ways of doing management.

19. Intercultural communication: Business negotiations in Romania

Owing to the country's history within the former Eastern Bloc until 1996, many businesspeople and officials in Romania may have only limited exposure to other cultures except for neighboring countries. Its culture is quite homogeneous. When negotiating business here, one should realize that people may expect things to be done "their way." However, some among younger generations may have greater international experience and can be open-minded. We highlight some of the main aspects of negotiating in business in Romania.

The negotiation dealt with the sale of a large number of digital cameras by the Japanese company to the Romanian one, over a period of 3 years. Mr. Popescu, president of the marketing division of the Romanian company, was selected to conduct this negotiation, due to his experience in dealing with other cultures, mostly American. The Romanian team arrived at the Japanese company 15 minutes prior to their appointment, which is very fortunate as Japan is a monochronic culture when doing business and punctuality is highly valued.

The meeting starts with everybody introducing themselves, shaking hands (the Romanians) and bowing (the Japanese). Mr. Popescu is the only one who bows instead of shaking hands. Nevertheless, the Japanese do not seem bothered by this, as in some cases they were the ones to offer their hands after bowing in front of the Romanian party. After the first introductions are concluded, the Japanese move on to the next logical step in the negotiation: rapport building. In this respect, both countries are relationship oriented and take time in small "chit-chat" as an icebreaker in the business meeting. However, the Romanian and Japanese definition of small talk differs in length. The Romanians are ready to give an answer to Mr. Yamada's question, but Mr. Dima considers the question "Are you tired?" as the perfect opening that leads into the business transaction itself: "Thank you for your concern. We are more than ready to discuss and we wanted to start with the letter of the 18th... What we would like to know...”

The Japanese considered this abrupt interruption of phatic communication as an outright refusal of *amae*. In the introductory stage, the Japanese try to find out how much *amae* (interdependence) and, of course, trust can be developed in the future business relationship. If *amae* is denied, there is little chance for trust to be established between the parties. Also, *amae* is closely linked to the *uchi* dimension, or, in other words, how quickly (if ever) the business partners will stop being outsiders *(soto)* and become part of the inside *(uchi)* group.

From then on, things seem to go from bad to worse. A middle ground of understanding cannot be settled, and the Romanian team monopolizes the conversation, in a feeble attempt to make the Japanese disclose their position and their thoughts.

All throughout the negotiation, the Japanese seem to employ avoidance strategies, by keeping silent and waiting before acting (wait and see). They refuse to make eye contact, their faces being down turned, with long silences (from 30 seconds up to 2 minutes) to express disagreement or to simply consider the proposal.

At first, the Romanians are under the impression that they did not make themselves properly understood, so what they do is to keep repeating and rephrasing the first request, waiting for an answer. When the Japanese's response is still to remain silent, the Romanians fall into the trap of readjusting their position. This quick concession on their part does not help their position, for it only reassures the Japanese that the price they offer can still be negotiated and increased in their favor. Therefore, seeing that their strategy is working, the Japanese continue to do what they do best: wait and see.

The Romanians, instead of waiting out the Japanese negotiators' periods of silence, pressure them into giving an answer, any kind of answer at this point. The Romanians are obviously uncomfortable with such long periods of silence and this puts them at a disadvantage, while the Japanese will fully take advantage of their discomfort and need to fill the voids in the conversation. From the Japanese perspective, they are just trying to keep the wa (harmony) in balance, which means they avoid saying "no" directly, out of concern for the social face of the other party. Thus, they give very vague "yes," which does not express agreement but only commitment for the interaction. (From "BUSINESS NEGOTIATIONS BETWEEN THE ROMANIANS AND THE JAPANESE—A CROSS-CULTURAL PERSPECTIVE" by Lavinia PETRE and Ruxandra CONSTANTINESCU-ŞTEFĂNEL. SYNERGY volume 8, no. 2/2012).

Attitudes and Styles—To Romanians, negotiating is usually a joint problem-solving process. While the buyer is in a superior position, both sides in a business deal share the responsibility to reach agreement. Although the primary negotiation style is competitive, Romanians, nevertheless, value long-term relationships and look for win-win solutions. They avoid any open confrontation as it could damage relationships. It is best to remain calm, friendly, patient, and persistent, never taking anything personally.

Should a dispute arise at any stage of a negotiation, you might be able to reach resolution by focusing on logical arguments and facts. In extreme situations, use a mediator, ideally the party who initially introduced you.

Sharing of Information—Romanian negotiators usually play their cards close to the chest, although some may share information as a way to build trust.

Keep in mind that humility is a virtue in Romanian business culture. If you make exaggerated claims in an effort to impress the other side or to obtain concessions, they will likely investigate your claims before responding.

Pace of Negotiation—Expect negotiations to be slow and protracted. Relationship building, information gathering, bargaining, and decision making may all take considerable time. Be prepared to make several trips if necessary to achieve your objectives. Throughout the negotiation, be patient, show little emotion, and accept that delays occur.

Romanians generally employ a polychronic work style. They are used to pursuing multiple actions and goals in parallel. When negotiating, they often take a holistic approach and may jump back and forth between topics rather than addressing them in sequential order. Negotiators from strongly monochronic cultures, such as Germany, the United Kingdom, or the United States, may find this style confusing, irritating, and even annoying. In any case, do not show irritation or anger when encountering this behavior. Instead, keep track of the bargaining progress at all times, often emphasizing areas where agreement already exists.

Bargaining—While businesspeople in the country may have learned the ground rules of international negotiations, their experience is usually limited. They are used to bargaining but not overly fond of haggling. However, Romanians can be tough and persistent negotiators, and it may be difficult to obtain concessions from them. The bargaining stage of a negotiation can be extensive.

Though concessions never come easily, prices may move by about 25 to 40 percent between initial offers and final agreement.

Deceptive techniques are frequently used. This includes tactics such as telling lies and sending fake non-verbal messages, pretending to be disinterested in the whole deal or in single concessions, or misrepresenting an item's value. Romanians may play stupid or otherwise attempt to mislead you in order to obtain bargaining advantages.

Negotiators in Romania may use pressure techniques that include silence, making final offers, or nibbling. Romanian negotiators avoid using overly aggressive or adversarial techniques.

As in most strongly relationship-oriented cultures, negotiators may sometimes use emotional techniques such as attitudinal bargaining, attempting to make you feel guilty, grimacing, or appealing to personal relationships.

As the country has moved from a socialist country to a free-market economy, corruption and bribery have become quite common in Romania's public and private sectors. However, people may draw the line differently, viewing minor payments as rewards for getting a job done rather than as bribes.

Also, keep in mind that there is a fine line between giving gifts and bribing. What you may consider a bribe, a Romanian may view as only a nice gift.

Decision Making—Companies are often very hierarchical, and people expect to work within clearly established lines of authority. Openly disagreeing with or criticizing superiors is unacceptable. Decision makers are primarily senior managers who consider the best interest of the group or organization. They rarely delegate their authority to lower levels in the hierarchy, but others are often consulted in a committee-style process in order to reach greater consensus over and support of the decision. This process can take a long time and requires patience. Romanians usually indicate it if they are not interested in doing business.

When making decisions, businesspeople may not rely much on rules or laws. They usually consider the specific situation rather than applying universal principles. Romanians are often reluctant to take risks. If you expect them to support a risky decision, you may need to find ways for them to become comfortable with it first, for instance by explaining contingency plans, outlining areas of additional support, or by offering guarantees and warranties.

Agreements and Contracts—Exchanging written understandings after meetings and at key negotiation stages is useful. Oral commitments may sound stronger than what your Romanian counterparts may be willing to put in writing. However, these documents are not final agreements. Any part of an agreement may still change significantly before both parties sign the final contract.

Written contracts tend to be lengthy. They often spell out detailed terms and conditions for the core agreements as well as for many eventualities. Signing the contract is important not only from a legal perspective, but also as a strong confirmation of your Romanian partners' commitment.

Although your legal rights may not always be enforceable, you should consult a local legal expert before signing a contract. For the time being, it is wise to recognize that the country's legal system is in a transitional mode, so be prepared for laws to change on short notice.

Signed contracts may not always be honored. This depends on the strength of the continuing relationship between the contract partners. It is strongly advisable to continue staying in touch and maintaining the trust of your Romanian business partner. Business partners usually expect the other side to remain somewhat flexible if conditions change, which may include agreeing to modify contract terms.

P.S. **There were several mistakes made in this negotiation:**

First, the Romanians acted less as a team than the Japanese. They seemed to take decisions individually, while the Japanese conferred every time there was a new issue raised.

Secondly, both cultures observed more their own norms and showed a lack of tolerance towards the other party's culture (the Romanian discussion about fairness because business is done in a certain way in Romania; the Japanese refusal to move to a first-name basis).

Thirdly, the Romanians' discomfort with silence put them in a very disadvantageous position as the Japanese manifested this behavior all throughout the negotiation.

As a result, they continued to change their position and make concessions just to cover the long moments of silence. The Romanians appeared to be inconstant because of the frequent change in position and requirements.

20. Buying a business in Romania: cultural due diligence and hidden cultural rules

Cross-border mergers and acquisitions are common and often used to acquire more efficient access to resources and human capital, to expand markets and to create new ones. Due to promising predictions, as well as a considerable amount of time and money spent on legal and administrative issues, potential difficulties deriving from cross-cultural differences and hidden cultural rules are often neglected. We will look at an actual acquisition of a Romanian business and analyze its impact.

Three years ago, Heineken N.V. announced the acquisition of the Romanian brewery Bere-Mureș. This transaction would strengthen Heineken's leadership in Romania increasing both its market share—31 percent, and volume to 6 million hectoliters.

"This transaction allows us to consolidate our leading position in Romania. We have a stronger portfolio, more diversified with leading brands and an excellent platform through which we will bring the value and development," commented Nico Nusmeier, Regional President of Heineken for Central and Eastern Europe.

The beer market in Romania was 90 percent controlled by five players—Ursus Breweries, Heineken, Bergenbier, Tuborg and Romaqua, while small producers accounted for only 10 percent of the market.

What was the reasoning behind the Heineken—Bere-Mureş deal? The two main players were forced to play the game of market leaders, as an alternative to organic growth, and any strategic movement like M&A was a key determinant in their market positioning. The particular case of Bere-Mureş acquisition was not necessarily a desired acquisition, but rather a reactive movement to the market tendencies.

In their turn, the Bere-Mureş shareholders sold the company simply because it was the best moment of exiting the market.

On the other hand, the main players Ursus and Heineken, fighting for the first position, were forced to get involved in the process and make a decision. At the moment of the acquisition the market share difference between Heineken and its main competitor SAB Miller was only 1 percentage point, thus the fight of getting Bere-Mureş that accounted for 6 percent of the market was very tight with both players negotiating in parallel with Bere-Mureş. The improvement in competitive position is one of the main drivers of M&A transactions and this was also one of the main reasons behind the Bere-Mureş acquisition.

During the process the two companies used a system called Total Product Management, which is very similar with Six Sigma concept, where Six Sigma can deal with a cultural change as well. "It was necessary to align all the processes of Bere-Mureş with those of Heineken Romania," said Vasile Ciurba, Member of the Board of Directors of Bere-Mureş.

Another aspect that was considered important was "the leadership style of the Romanian management of Bere-Mureş, which was a direct leadership style, the decisions were taken much faster compared to Heineken Romania." Two different national cultures (NC)—collectivist and individualistic ones, were merged into a new organizational culture (OC) through successful leadership.

There are various obstacles for international mergers and acquisitions and these can have a tremendous impact on the international workforce and global business operations if not addressed in the early stages.

Growth Strategy =>Potential Targets => Due Diligence => Cultural Integration => "One" Business => Develop and Sustain

Obstacles for international M&A in the cultural field include:

– different values,

– attitudes and behavior between the home and the host culture which can cause misunderstandings,

– client and employee dissatisfaction.

Cultural due diligence

The cultural fit between an acquirer and a target is one of the most neglected areas of analysis prior to the closing of a deal. However, cultural due diligence is as important as careful financial analysis. Without it, the chances are great that M&A will quickly amount to misunderstanding, confusion and conflict. **Cultural due diligence involves steps** like: determining the importance of culture, assessing the culture of both— a target and an acquirer.

It is useful to know the target management behavior with respect to dimensions such as centralized versus decentralized decision making, speed in decision making, time horizon for decisions, level of team work, management of conflict, risk orientation, openness to change, communication styles etc.

It is necessary to assess the cultural fit between the acquirer and target based on cultural profile. Potential sources of clash must be managed. It is necessary to identify the impact of cultural gap, and develop and execute strategies to use the information in the cultural profile to assess the impact that the differences have.

The Cultural Assessment starts with asking the right questions

1. How does cultural integration planning fit into acquisition strategic planning, negotiation, and due diligence processes?

2. How can executives identify critical implementation issues during the planning and negotiation stages?

3. What integration tools are useful for functional departments? For merged cross-functional

projects? For individuals and multicultural small task groups who must work together for the first time?

4. What are the roles of top (from one culture) and mid-level (from another culture) management (on both sides) during implementation?

Answers to these questions will help leaders/ managers get an idea of what to expect during the merger and how do deal with the specific cultural issues.

Recommendations

More broadly, the challenges of changing from a single, culturally integrated national organization operating in a familiar market in one time zone to managing a cross-border organization incorporating a new set of people, perspectives and issues can take many management teams by surprise.

Set clear expectations and invest in high-quality, two-way communication. Recognizing and adapting to the different communication styles and expectations of the cultures involved will also help to reduce any feelings of mistrust and concern—not only among employees but, just as importantly, among clients and other stakeholders in the new markets.

Acknowledge cultural differences but simultaneously create a common corporate culture with a single goal: achieving high performance. Successful cross-border M&As are often those that embrace cultural diversity as a creative and fertile source of positive new "ways of doing things" and go on to create a "third culture" that is shared by all employees and embraced by external stakeholders. Awareness of language, cultural values, attitudes and behaviors are critical success factors of the integration process.

Move to a cross-border operating model. Through integrated management. Cultural differences between organizations of different nationalities could affect the suitability of prospective partners and the management style to be adopted should the alliance or takeover proceed.

21. Ethnic entrepreneurship in Romania: Turkish business development

Romania, which displays an ethnic minority diversity, can offer a real and sustainable model of multicultural co-existence. Turkish entrepreneurs were part of an early wave of entrepreneurs in post-communist Romania, and may have played an important part in shaping business in the country.

Turkey's largest diary producer, Sütaş, has taken its second step in the Balkans by acquiring a factory in Romania as it looks to enter European markets using the region as a base.

Sütaş, which recently bought a dairy production facility in the Macedonian city of Skopje, announced that it has taken over a factory in Bucharest that had belonged to an Israeli dairy producer.

"We're delighted to make our second investment in the Balkans with Romania. As our Romania facility becomes operational, we aim to access European Union markets," Muharrem Yılmaz, the chairman of the board of Sütaş, said in a statement.

The facility in Romania has a daily capacity of 500 tons, and the Turkish company hopes to cooperate with related institutions in Romania to improve the conditions of milk production there. Sütaş aims to provide employment for 300 people directly in one year and raise this amount to 500 after its investments are completed. "Considering the indirect employment that the sector creates in the agriculture, logistics and services, Sütaş's investment will have a substantial impact on production, employment and income distribution in the region," Yılmaz said."

There is a long history of Romanian and Turkish relationships and Turkish entrepreneurs were among the first to develop business in Romania in the early 1990s. At that time Romania already had a significant Turkish community in Dobrogea, which served as a bridge between the two countries.

Turkish entrepreneurs have made a significant contribution to the transition to a market economy, as well as to economic recovery, in post-1989 Romania. A very important aspect of this is their support to creating an entrepreneurial culture in Romania, based on their successful integration in the Romanian economy whilst preserving their cultural identity and respecting the basic values of Romanian society.

Starting from the early 1990s, the phenomenon of immigration, mainly for economic and political reasons, contributed to an increase in multiculturalism in Romania. For a country such as Romania, which did not experience large scale immigration in the past, it has become important to prepare for the challenges brought by immigration and to anticipate possible tensions based on ethnicity and religion. At the same time, Turkish entrepreneurs offer a model of ethnic entrepreneurship able to increase opportunities for a more entrepreneurial Romania, combined with a model of successful integration of ethnic groups into its society.

Turkey provided entrepreneurs in two waves:

The first wave, arriving soon after 1990 (a few thousand), with modest capital, started small ventures (bakeries, textile boutiques, etc.). The firms' financing was based on informal sources, such as personal savings, loans from family and friends, home equity loans. They sent positive feedback regarding the Romanian business environment, the civil society's open attitude, the tolerance toward foreign entrepreneurs.

The second, more consistent wave, followed few years later, encouraged by the successes of the first wave of entrepreneurs. These were the so called Euro-Turks. Resident in the EU, these immigrant entrepreneurs were highly motivated, usually had previous experience in the venture field and more developed financial skills, which, combined with the Romanian market opportunities, have been key to their business success. As these entrepreneurs have got involved in a large variety of economic sectors (retail, wholesale, manufacturing, finance, services, etc.), they have brought about an important qualitative change in the Turkish entrepreneurship phenomenon in Romania.

The highest concentration of Turkish entrepreneurs can be noticed in Bucharest, the rest of being widely spread across mainly in urban areas (Constanța, Brașov, Pitești, Craiova, Cluj-Napoca, Timișoara). It is useful to underline that the small Turkish companies established all over the country, including in rural areas, were a sign of successful break-out strategies and also a proof of high tolerance and acceptance on by the Romanian population.

As a result, Romania has become the largest recipient of Turkish direct investment in this region. Turkish entrepreneurs do not discriminate on ethnic grounds when hiring: The majority of the personnel they hire are not Turkish. This open attitude offers the chance to strengthen communication and other forms of interaction with the majority of the population.

The integration of Turkish entrepreneurs in civil society is made smooth by networks of several professional associations, ethnic and religion-based organizations with strong connections at national and international level.

The Turkish Businessmen Association (TIAD) is one of the most dynamic organizations. It is involved in supporting the economic activities of its members in the "Romanian friendly environment."

An intense cooperation was established between TIAD and the two leading minority organizations (the Democratic Union of Turkish-Muslims Tartars in Romania and the Turks' Democratic Union in Romania) in order to support social, religious and cultural projects concerning the whole Turkish community. Cultural events have been organized in close cooperation with other ethnic organizations and the

Department for Inter-ethnic Relations, aiming to enhance unity, peace and stability among minorities.

A subtle factor impacting Turkish entrepreneurship in Romania is religion. Even if they belong to different main religious denominations, Romania and Turkey generally show little differences with respect to people's opinions on religious beliefs and practice. Religious freedom in both Romania and Turkey is a constitutional right and the relations are generally amicable between different religions. However, international studies indicate that a greater religious freedom exists in Romania, which can positively influence the entrepreneurial decisions.

The Turks' Muslim religious background is significantly different in cultural terms when compared with the majority's Orthodox Christian religion in Romania. At the same time, "Turkish Muslims are, in comparison with other Islamic people, more flexible and therefore more open and reform-oriented."

An undeniable proof in that sense is Turkish women's involvement in business. Approximately 20% of all Turkish companies in Romania are entirely or partially owned by women. Four of them are TIAD members.

Social and business relationships provide women entrepreneurs with information and easier access to resources, and shape expectations for new ventures and venture financing. Turkish women entrepreneurs also settle a good example of access to professional life, raising awareness among both Turkish and Romanian women.

The positive impact of ethnic entrepreneurship, especially in the urban areas, with a predominantly external orientation, consists of social bonds in a cultural network, which create flexible ways to attract personnel and capital, the potential of organizing businesses at the interface of own and host cultures and the capacity to generate market niches for specific cultural goods. It also brings an important contribution to reducing social exclusion and raising living standards in ethnic groups. Moreover, when ethnic minorities and ethnic entrepreneurs concentrate in particular localities, they can influence the development of local economies as a whole and the standard of living within them.

The smooth integration of the Turkish community, in general and that of Turkish entrepreneurs, in particular, despite different traditions and religious background, is a successful example. Turkish entrepreneurs have not encountered serious barriers in Romania as compared to other EU countries.

Romania is becoming increasingly attractive for the Turks settled for decades in Western Europe as well, and this can determine a growing share of Turkish capital as well as a raising the quality of entrepreneurial culture in the Romanian economy.

22. In food we trust: a story of Irish and Romanians working together

For a foreigner, opening a restaurant in Romania is a complex intercultural exercise. Dealing with local staff and local customers, while serving food from another culture—that's something worth looking into.

Food is only one aspect of cultural traditions, yet it is probably one of the most persistent. There is no cultural group and no individual for whom at least one specific food—the memory, taste, or smell of which—does not evoke a pang of loving nostalgia. Food forms an inextricable part in our daily lives. Without food we cannot survive. But it is much more than a necessity. Food is a source of pleasure, comfort and security. Food is also a symbol of hospitality, social status, and religious significance. What we select to eat, how we prepare it, serve it, and even how we eat it are all factors profoundly touched by our individual cultural inheritance.

If you want to open a restaurant in a country different from yours—keep it in mind!

Peoples of differing cultures share most countries in the world. The human habit of migrating is as old as the history of humans. It is accepted that people move from place to place for reasons of religious or political freedom, for personal and family security, for a sense of adventure. What is often overlooked is something more basic; many peoples of the world have migrated to find food. Historically, this has frequently resulted in the necessity of relinquishing customary tastes according to what foods, seasonings, and even cooking methods are available to them in the new location. Finding new foods and new sources of foods and seasonings also motivated many adventurers and explorers and swelled the economy of countries.

John McCarthy, an Irish businessman with a background in landscaping, moved to Romania many years ago. And opened his own business—the Malagamba restaurant located in Lipscani, the old historic center of Bucharest. I met him and was interested in the intercultural issues—an Irish owner of business, Romanian staff and Italian cuisine.

Irish people have a reputation for ease and elegance of speech and readiness to put things into practice. More importance and weight are given to the spoken than to the written word.

Irish people have more flexible approach to organization than, for example, British people. This is reflected in the importance given to personal relationships, a talent for improvisation and a dislike of rigid systems and bureaucracy. Sounds encouraging, doesn't it?

Irish are essentially cooperative and work well in teams. Teams do not necessarily need a strong leader, but if they have one they should make sure that they are part of the team and do not stand apart. Teams will commonly accept collective responsibility for decisions and implementations. Active consensus in decisions is usually desirable. Irish are known to be direct. Important discussions and decisions often take place in an informal environment outside the office.

During the meeting, John kept an eye on his staff in between the meals, commenting on served bread, soup or the temperature of table water right there, on the spot. It looked more like a friendly meeting than a business one for the staff. I was the witness of the dialogue between the owner and a waiter about the served coffee or, to be exact, about the way this coffee was made—too many bubbles for a cup of espresso! Who cares about bubbles in espresso? The Irish owner did!

But what was more important is the attitude of the Romanian waiter. Romanians are known for conflict avoidance and quiet intonation during inter-actions. Any raised voice would insult them and put at a distance! Just keep the mouth shut and wait. Not in this case. The waiter smiled and said that she would ask the bartender to calibrate the coffee machine.

The turnover of staff at the beginning was very high. Lack of loyalty, professional skills, crisis and change management skills were the reasons for firing people every week. But things changed for the good and in the last two years there was no turnover at all. "We are in the same team," was John McCarthy's message to the staff. "It is not easy to be a waiter or a bartender. It is very multitasking, not to mention physical, job! You need to remember each client's requests and orders, its consequences and require-ments. Clients and guests are supposed to leave with an easy and warm feeling, while waiters should finish their day with a strong muscle tension. Meaning the job has been done," he says.

Many Irish traditional values seem to be com-mon for Romanians: rural simplicity, vision and imagination, romance and idealism, irony and sense of humor, informality, poetic tendencies, love of literature, music, theatre, warmth and charm, social anchors of land, church, family...

Irish people are not great agenda followers, ideas are more important than plain facts. The Irish have a strong affinity for the abstract, innovative, theoretical. They look at new ways of approaching problems and tasks. Which leads to creativity. They are unconventional and independent spirits who resist structure and routine. And Latins (Romanians) find it easy to accept!

The restaurant is named after Sergiu Malagamba, a Romanian jazz composer!

23. Marketing across cultures: why the "American ROM" campaign for Romanian chocolate bar worked

Culturally-aware marketers can make the difference when it comes to failing or succeeding on a certain market. Products that are adapted to the traits of a culture are those that stand more changes of being picked up from the shelves. How should companies create their marketing strategies for Romania?

McCann Erickson Romania got the Grand Prix at the Cannes Lions International Festival of Creativity this year for its "American ROM" campaign for candy makers Kandia Dulce. The producers of chocolate bar, which is usually decorated with the Romanian flag, wanted to appeal to the youth disenchanted by the country's economic and political problems. This example is a lesson in itself. What other similar campaign, or shifts in marketing to cater to Romanian cultural needs have you heard of? So they put an American flag on the packaging instead, and created an English ad campaign where an American executive boasts about the switch. It sparked a dialogue and a swelling of Romanian pride—exactly what the company was hoping for—before turning the packaging back to its original form.

When we begin to include other cultures as either—or as both—buyers and sellers, basic models not only fail the marketer because of cultural differences, but an entirely different logic is required. Culture is not simply another factor in marketing mix, but must be seen in the context of all transactions. It changes the entire landscape that pervades all relationships and behaviors and, importantly, "meaning."

Culture challenges the fundamental strategy of marketing, customer relations, definition of product, price, and advertisement. In short, culture is all pervading.

However, much more important than these obvious aspects of culture, are differences that derive from the different meaning given by different cultures to the same thing.

For example, Americans may purchase a music player because it enables them to "listen to their favorite music without being disturbed by others." The

Japanese may purchase the same product in order to "listen to their favorite music without disturbing others."

The product may be technically identical, but the purchase motive is different, because of the different meanings and priorities given to oneself and others' privacy.

Kodak introduced an advertising campaign based on capturing "memories" in the physical form of photographs. In contrast, for European cultures, "memory" is a much more sentimental construct and may be tainted if represented in the explicit format of a photograph that omits the higher levels of the experience. Procter & Gamble have successfully developed a new generation of highly absorbent Pampers with the unique selling point that they can be changed less frequently. This approach failed in Japan where frequent changing of diapers/nappies is perceived as fundamental to keeping the baby clean.

Organizations need stability and change, tradition and innovation, public and private interest, planning, order and freedom, growth and decay. Successful marketers must deal with these issues.

Recognize—Whilst we can more easily recognize explicit cultural differences, we may not be aware of implicit cultural differences. The first step is to recognize that there are cultural differences.

Respect—Different orientations about "where I am coming from" are not "right or wrong," they are just different. It is all too easy to be judgmental about people and societies that give different meaning to their world from ours. Thus, the next step is to respect these differences and accept customers' rights to interpret the world (and our products and marketing efforts) in the way they choose.

Reconcile—Because of these different views of the world, the marketer can encounter two seemingly opposing views of the contrasting cultures—those of the seller and buyer. The task of the marketer is to reconcile these seemingly opposing differences.

The question is, should we have one standardized approach (identical product range and associated identical marketing support) or should we go for a local approach (different products and local based marketing in each destination)? Do we think our customers are best served by becoming nearly globally universal and alike, or by becoming more influenced by particular national or local cultures?

The answer lies in transnational specialization. Here we reconcile the seemingly opposing extremes. We integrate best practice and satisfy customer needs by learning from the diversity of adopting, adapting, and combining the best.

MacDonalds successfully achieved this integration by branding the Big Mac universally across the globe. The big "M" sign, represents the universal corporate identity with standard furnishings and fittings in all their restaurants, including in Romania. Yet in the Middle East, the Big Mac is a veggie-burger, and served with rice rather than fries in the Asiatic.

In some situations, the marketing strength derives from the universal world branding. Thus, Coca-Cola is Coca-Cola everywhere and represents the American dream, although ingredient details on the can or bottle may be in a local language.

Similarly, British Airways are selling safe, reliable, quintessential "Englishness," supported by local agents in the different destinations it serves.

Is marketing concerned with satisfying individual customer needs and preferences, or is the focus placed on creating a trend or fashion that is adopted by the group? Individuals then purchase to show they have joined the group by following the shared trend.

From the customers perspective, do we relate to others by discovering what each one of us individually wants, or do we place ahead of this some shared concept to which we can identify and feel part of?

Simply rejecting another's viewpoint or adopting a compromise does not yield the best market return. In our new marketing paradigm, we can follow the reconciliation logic by starting from one extreme, but integrating with the needs of the other one.

This means that, although marketing to an individualistic culture (ex., Scandinavian countries) might see an individual as an end, marketing will benefit from a collective arrangement (ex., Romania) as the means to achieve that end. Conversely, marketing to a communitarian culture sees the group as the target market, yet can use feedback and suggested improvements from individuals.

The marketing relationship should be seen as circular. The decision to focus on one end is only arbitrary.

Microsoft Windows and its associated Office Products offer the benefits of a group approach. Documents can be shared and exchanged, because they adhere to common file formats. Yet individuals can tailor the configuration of their system to satisfy individual preferences—such as the screen zoom level to meet their individual eyesight capabilities.

Jaguar and Mercedes owner-drivers take pride in being a member of their fellow club of drivers of prestige cars (belonging to their peer group). However, when they insert their individual key in the lock of their own car, the seats and driving mirror configures to their own preference, even though some else may have altered these settings.

What is the degree of involvement of the customer?

Do we see the customer as a "catch," someone from who we can make fast money, or is the customer a relationship, involving a series of transactions over time. Do we need a relationship first, before he/she becomes a customer, or do we easily do business, from which a relationship may or not follow?

Marketing through Reconciliation is more than this compromise. It is the craft of trying to define those specific areas to provide a more personal service and, thereby, deepen the relationship. The future success of a seller-buyer alliance will depend on one particular reconciliation: the competency of the marketing team to identify those specific circumstances where specific moments can be used to deepen the relationship in the provided service.

What part does the display and role of emotion play, and/or is the display of emotion controlled?

Typically, reason and emotion are linked or combined. When the customer expresses satisfaction (or dissatisfaction!), they are trying to find confirmation in their thoughts and feelings—and trying to show they have the same response as others. ("I have the same view of this product/service as you.") Customers whose response is neutral are seeking an indirect response.

Do we sell function or status?

Does the customer want a functional product that achieves the utilitarian purpose or are they buying status? You can tell the time from a 1 euro LED digital watch as well as with a 10,000 Euros Rolex Oyster. But a Rolex Oyster is a symbolic representation of status, not simply a watch. All societies give certain members higher status than others, signaling that unusual attention should be focused on those persons and the products they own and display and the services they consume.

In achievement-oriented cultures, the emphasis is on performance. In ascribed-status cultures, such as Asia, status is ascribed to products that naturally evoke admiration from others, such as high technology and jewelery. The status is less concerned with the functional capabilities of the product.

This dilemma between the achieved and ascribed status can be seen in the profit-oriented versus non-profit status of the private health care companies in Romania. Should the pharma company set a goal of

25% profit to shareholders to compete on the stock exchange or make just enough return to serve the sick and the weak? To care about people you serve is a precursor to success and you must ascribe status to them. The provident status reconciles the need to achieve business growth with providing primary health care. Care for your employees through a strong successful business base and they pass that care to the clients (patients).

Technology Push or Market Pull?

Are we stimulated by an inner drive, or do we adapt to external events that are beyond our control? The main issue here is to connect the internally controlled culture of technology push (sell what we can make) with the externally controlled world of market pull (make what we can sell).

Nobody will deny the great knowledge and inventiveness of Nokia, separately, of its technologies and the quality of its marketing. The problem is that these two major areas didn't seem to connect. The push of the technology needs to help you decide what markets you want to be pulled by, and the pull of the market needs to help you know what technologies to push.

This dilemma was not properly reconciled by Nokia which left Romania in 2011.

Do we view time as sequential or synchronic?

With sequential cultures, time is an objective measure of passing increments. The faster you can act and get to the market, there more effective will be your competitiveness. In contrast, synchronous cultures, like doing things "just in time," and so that present ideas converge on the future. The better your timing, the more competitive you will be (where do you think Romania is...?)

Keeping traditional products that made your name in the first place can jeopardize the creation of new products. Heineken successfully integrated the (past) traditions of the Heineken family with the future needs of the company, and the traditions of the Heineken product with the need for (future) innovation—for example in the area of beers. Process innovation sought new methods of creating the same result (traditional product), whilst product innovation allowed new drinks from scratch without involving Heineken's premium product in the experiments.

This Marketing paradigm thus requires a mindset that recognizes cultural differences, respects these differences and then reconciles the continuing dilemmas. It needs to include the system of activities, which facilitates human interaction and information between products/services on the one hand and markets on the other.

What are the main traits of the Romanian culture that marketers should take into account when creating their strategies for this market? What do you think?

24. Modern Austrian business society and old traditions at play in Romania: the Viennese Ball

Austrians want to protect their national identity and remain in many ways a closed and introverted society. In Austria there is a historical respect for aristocrats, not unrelated to the nostalgia felt for the old empire. The Viennese Ball in Bucharest is one of the examples of a synthesis between modern Austrian business society and old traditions.

The Viennese Ball in Bucharest is one of the examples combining the features of a modern Austrian business society and old traditions.

At the heart of Austrian business life is the concept known as Sozialpartnerschaft—social partnership—based on a comprehensive system of chambers and associations, business and professional clubs. Membership is mandatory. There is a deep sense of community, which embraces the sense of belonging and mutual responsibility between companies and their employees. Loyalty and conservatism are also reflected in outside business relationships. It is difficult to break into existing supplier arrangements and then only if the type and standard of service are radically different.

Having a similar tradition in both countries—Romania and Austria—balls are a strong networking tradition where another Austrian trait for formality is lightly counterbalanced by an easy-going approach to life. The quality that Austrians value most in their social life and their personal relations at work is Gemütlichkeit, best described as a comfortable geniality. Photos of the Viennese Ball in Bucharest reveal old world elegance combined with a sense of informality.

Traditionally, Austria's ball season starts on November 11th at 11:11 and ends 40 days before Easter, giving Vienna a fairytale like atmosphere—the elegant, spectacular, well-mannered capital of the world.

The oldest and best known events of this type are: the famous Opernball, the Opera Ball, taking place at the Staatsoper, the Kaiserball (Imperial Ball) on December 31, at the Hofburg Imperial Palace, the Ball der Wiener Philharmoniker (Ball of the Vienna Philharmonic orchestra), a classy event in the building of the Musikverein, the Gala der Wiener Wirtschaft (Gala of the Viennese Industry) at the Hofburg Imperial Palace, and the Juristenball (Lawyers' Ball), one of the more upper-class balls, also in the Hofburg.

However it has also become customary that classical Viennese Balls are regularly organized outside of Austria, as for instance in New York, Washington, Moscow, London, Melbourne and not to forget the annual Viennese Ball in Bucharest. The first Viennese Ball was organized in Bucharest in 2006.

The grand ball, as a social event, was adopted by the Bucharest elite in the 19th century. The custom caught on so quickly that balls and receptions were soon competing in number, opulence and brilliance. Both foreign guests and Romanians agreed that among the grandest balls and receptions held in Bucharest in the mid-19th century were those hosted by Madame Oteteleșanu and by Princess Irina Grigore Șuțu. Most appreciable were those organized by Șuțu, Știrbei and Bibescu.

Apart from the balls organized by important houses, another two fashionable events were on going by the time: The Jockey-Club and the Obolul-Club. The Jockey-Club ball, reserved for women and young ladies of the club and a reduced member of invited was regarded as "chic." The Obolul ball, as a public fund-raising event, was held in the National Theatre hall.

Austrian leadership style is autocratic and authoritarian, which helped refresh this tradition in Romania. "Knowing the right people" is another strong point similar to Romanian business culture. At the same time Austrians are prepared to claim personal responsibility for decisions that in a collectivist culture like Romania would be ascribed to a team.

Many Austrians speak good English, although they stick to German wherever possible, even in a multicultural context. They have a factual, numerate and direct approach to communication that is intolerant to euphemism and allusion. Though directness and frankness can be sweetened by charm. The PR campaign for the Viennese Ball can be another confirmation of this type of communication.

This word "charm" can crop up most often in discussing Austrian manners. There is an engaging cordiality and genuine hospitality about their manners. Courtesy goes deeper than mere politeness. Being always well dressed and presentable, generous and hospitable but distant and respected at the same time.

Bilateral relations between Austria and Romania may indeed be described as excellent and solid. One reason for this success can be found, certainly in the common history and cultural similarities.

25. Cultural differences in advertising: Romania and Brazil

Existing in a world where interaction between nations is extremely frequent, modern people have increasingly numerous channels for getting in touch with foreign culture. Acculturation therefore happens all the time because of the conjunction of two or more cultural systems. Since effective communication depends largely on the understanding of different cultures in a world economy, the role of culture in advertising is undoubtedly. In this story we're looking at the Romanian and Brazilian advertising markets.

A Romanian agency brought some creative Brazilians to the Romanian market. This triggered some comparison between the Romanian and the

Brazilian creative markets. In a nutshell, Romanian ads are very informative with words and celebrities associated with those words, while Brazilian ads are very visual, the message is in objects. But there's more to it.

Cultural aspects are particularly important in advertising since the effectiveness of messages transmitted via the mass media is determined mostly by the appropriateness of the words and other symbols they employ. Nowadays, understanding cultural differences is frequently considered a prerequisite for successful international advertising. The reasoning is that consumers grow up in a particular culture and hence become accustomed to the value systems, beliefs, and perception processes of that culture. Consequently consumers respond to advertising messages that are congruent with their culture, rewarding advertisers who understand that culture and tailor ads accordingly.

In Romania, ad agencies have creative ideas, but clients are mostly risk-averse and have the tendency to take the safer approach. A very good client service is required here in Romania, essentially convincing clients to buy ideas. In fact, there are a lot of interesting ideas in Romania, but they are implemented for a short time so they do not have a significant impact.

Brazil is different. Brazil enjoys an international reputation for producing some of the world's most creative advertising. The mere mention of Brazil to advertising professionals evokes images of innovative, appealing print ads and commercials—many that have taken top prizes at the Cannes Lions International Advertising Festival and other international competitions.

Successful advertising needs to incorporate functional as well as hedonistic benefits in order to induce positive attitudes amongst the target audience. A strategy pursued by agencies in Romania to target the elderly was to create advertisements that evoked pleasant memories from the communist system, for example. Anecdotal evidence and discussion with brand managers of multinationals in Romania highlighted that such campaigns enjoyed good rates of interest and induced positive attitudes toward the brand, stimulating the emotional stage according to the hierarchy of effects model.

On the other hand, Brazilian advertising tried to stay away from the past. Advertising began to address consumers in a more colloquial voice rather than continuing the more formal language used in the past. This brought advertising closer to consumers and they responded positively to ads that spoke to them like they talk to their friends. This new style can be described as very engaging, humorous, and "very Brazilian."

Emotions and prior beliefs can be used to induce positive attitudes to advertising and emulate favorable attitudes toward brands. Brazilian advertisers seem to have an easier life in that sense. Generally speaking, Brazilians like and admire advertising, especially when it is entertaining. It is accepted and tolerated to a much higher degree than anywhere else. Marcio Moreira, Vice Chairman and Chief Talent Officer of McCann World group, and native Brazilian, puts it this way: "The Brazilian public is a sucker for advertising! The cynicism, the skepticism, the questioning, the 'I don't buy that' attitude is still not there. It's an environment in which advertising people are stars."

In Romania, advertising is still controversial. It is obvious that the perception of positive effects is decreasing compared to 2002, which brings challenges to the advertising industry, that has to continually reinvent itself, according to Traian Năstase, Online Project Manager, GfK Romania.

The same situation also applies to the degree to which ads succeed in being funny. If the number of those who believe that advertising is often fun is decreasing (from two-thirds in 2002 to 58 percent in

2011), an exception to this rule are the inhabitants of Bucharest. Advertisers are striving for more attention by trying different approaches.

Advertising is ubiquitous in Brazil. Familiar venues for advertising include television, billboards and signs in city streets, magazines, newspapers, and electronic media. Evening soap operas *(telenovelas)* are extremely popular and, along with sporting events, especially soccer, provide some of the most coveted advertising space.

The most popular programming continues to be the evening news and the soap operas that run at 7 and 8 o'clock. It is difficult to overstate the loyalty to and interest in the *telenovela* (soap opera) in Brazil. Whole families arrange their days so as not to miss the nightly episodes. The associated commercial slots form nearly perfect media opportunities for advertisers. In addition, many products are used and talked about in the soap operas themselves, making product placement a familiar and highly successful marketing device. Other great loves of the Brazilian people are soccer and carnival—both of which create important advertising venues as well.

In Romania, the global economic crisis that started in the fall of 2008 has been a cold shower. The sharp decline in advertising came at a moment when the media environment in Bucharest seemed to be expanding on many levels. However, the sharp decrease in advertising revenue is not the only reason for the crisis affecting the media industry in Romania. As a matter of fact, the signs that something was not working quite right had been visible for a good while for the keen eye. Despite the increase in advertising fuelled by the growing economy, the advertising pie had actually been diminishing for the print media.

The quality of content had also been getting weaker with publications trying to make up for lost readers by turning toward sensationalism, and printing fewer investigations, in-depth stories and other relevant information. TV and radio were also losing audiences, as people doing better economically used them less for escapism.

Going back to Brazil, during the 1970s and 1980s, the Brazilian market was generally closed to foreign imports. When it opened up in the 1990s—about the same time as Romania's market opened after the fall of communism, imported cars, wine, and other luxury goods from abroad became available. Multinational corporations began buying Brazilian businesses and using them to extend their global reach. As a consequence of this transformation of the Brazilian market, the advertising industry also changed.

But the foreign owners could not understand the language, humor, or style of Brazilian advertisements. Moreover, the multinationals wanted campaigns that would work throughout Latin America, not just in Portuguese-speaking Brazil. This linguistic block—the Portuguese language -precluded others understanding and admiring even the most brilliant copy. Moreover, puns, jokes, and other forms of language play did not translate well. Thus, Brazilian advertising became much more dependent on visual communication.

(The information about Advertising in Brazil is based on the book written by William O'Barr "Advertising and Society", 2008).

26. Intercultural: Team work with a fusion spin

Lets look how multi-cultural teams can apply fusion collaboration principles in order to get things done—and what obstacles they might find in the process.

Here are some team leaders who achieve the same result (getting the most out of all cultural subgroups) by carefully establishing team norms at the start of a project. For example, one manager who was leading an English-language software-development project and English was not his first language. In fact, his English was strongly accented. When he met with the team for the first time, he told them, 'You've probably noticed I have an accent. If I could get rid of it, I'd be happy to do so, but since I cannot, we're going to have to communicate... regardless of my accent or for that matter yours. If you do not understand me, or one another, whether it's because of accent or anything else, we need to communicate until we do understand (example from Janssens, Maddy and Jeanne M. Brett (2006), "Cultural Intelligence in global teams: A fusion model of collaboration")

In the United States, you will normally see communication styles that are time efficient, informal and direct. Not all countries practice direct confrontation and outside the United States, meeting styles such as ours can be seen as more aggressive than in other cultures.

In France, meetings are more heavily formatted with emphasis on hierarchy. The boss is rarely contradicted, so the key to success is to build consensus for an idea prior to a meeting. French executives value sophisticated language and communication skills.

Meetings in Brazil tend to emphasize relationship-building, using informal communication style, direct eye contact, bold body language, and passionate verbal communication. Team members prefer to know their defined roles and the details of the chain of command, while timing is less of an absolute.

Team members in China may be reluctant to go against the group because the culture is consensus driven and team oriented. Decision-making is best done after meetings in a series of discussions as team members are often reluctant to say "no" or go against the group.

And all these cultures meet in Romania for a project to be implemented in agricultural business.

When a French company prepared to merge with a Romanian firm, American and Romanian engineers discussed the difficulties of working with each other. As the Americans saw it, their Romanian colleagues took an "analysis paralysis" approach to problem solving: They insisted on analyzing the problem completely and correctly before taking any action.

The term "analysis paralysis" or "paralysis of analysis" refers to over-analyzing or over-thinking a situation, so that a decision or action is never taken, in effect paralyzing the outcome.

Americans, in the Romanian engineers' view, insisted on action from the start, often at the expense of fully understanding the problem.

Cultural disagreements of that type aren't necessarily insoluble. When an American software engineer started to work with a team of Israelis, for example, he was shocked by their argumentative approach—until he realized that they took the same approach to each other. He adapted by imposing some structure on the team's work, while allowing himself and his colleagues to express themselves naturally.

In another case, American and British members of a research team had violent disagreements over the speed at which they worked on a project. The Americans wanted to go full steam ahead while the Brits wished to advance more slowly in case they met serious pitfalls. Management accommodated both groups by setting an in-between speed that kept the project moving while allowing it to foresee problems.

And when a group of Chinese engineers encountered huge challenges cooperating with Brazil engineers on a project, they organized some training materials designed to stimulate the two groups to talk about their assumptions and experiences. The materials helped the two groups of engineers to understand each other's worldviews and to collaborate more effectively.

The Fusion Approach

We can summarize the strength of the fusion concept with a simple example. "Look at greeting behavior. Kissing, bowing, and shaking hands all achieve greeting effectively. In fusion, team members realize there's a different way of doing things over there and how the team can use those differences to be more creative."

The term "Fusion" is used here because of its resemblance to fusion cooking.

This culinary method combines or substitutes ingredients or cooking techniques from different cultural traditions while preserving their distinct flavors, textures, and presentations. Fusion cooking is a method that relies on combining different styles of cooking and cooking ingredients in such a way that the elements remain identifiable, but their juxtaposition is unique.

In similar fashion, the fusion approach to teamwork aims to obtain contributions from individual team members whenever those members' understanding or expertise is relevant to the team's goal.

In teamwork where a team consists of different cultures, fusion is based on two fundamental elements of collaboration: coexistence of differences and meaningful participation.

Fusion is an entirely new concept. It is not intuitive, because it is complex.

Multicultural teams have an obvious advantage over homogeneous teams: divergent thinking. Just as two heads are better than one, so two or more cultural perspectives should lead to more creative decisions and solutions. While homogeneous teams are good at reproducing solutions, heterogeneous teams are appropriate for solving new, complex problems.

Most multicultural teams collaborate in one of two ways. In the dominant (or subgroup) coalition model, a coalition of team members directs the extraction of information and the team's decision making. A dominant coalition does not necessarily consist of a majority of the team's members—it might be a minority group or even a single person. But whatever its constitution, it has power.

Alternatively, the integration and/or identity model requires team members to sublimate the identity of their own cultural groups to that of the entire team. They do so by adopting "superordinate goals" based on the common interests of team members. This process gives the team's entire membership broader access to information and decision making than the dominant coalition model. However members might yield some of their cultural identity—and hence their tendency to think differently—in the interests of unity. Also the team might function at the level of its least productive member. This lowest common denominator philosophy can dilute contributions from the most productive members.

How can teams ensure meaningful participation of members with the appropriate knowledge at the appropriate time? One of the ways to get people to participate is to make the size of the groups smaller, and to seed each small group with someone who is likely to support the team member who has not been participating.

To maintain its creativity as its tasks change, the team should continually reconstitute the subgroups. And whenever disagreements occur, as they inevitably will, members should take a vote. This approach preserves differences and gets decisions made.

But how does the fusion model fare if one cultural group consistently wins the votes and exerts its power in other ways? Here a team leader should make formal interventions to balance the power equation. Such interventions might aim at managing the team's time better. They might encourage more questioning among team members. Alternatively, the leader might appoint individuals or subgroups to work on a particular problem independently and then share their solutions with the entire team.

This collaboration will also teach and encourage Eastern European cultures to participate and speak up more in group problem-solving.

27. Intercultural: Cultural ethical dilemmas in business—from bribes paying to political affairs

What do we do with at certain ethical issues when it comes to business, from the bribe—known in Romania as *Șpaga*—to ethical issues in political affairs.

Ethics is an important part of our business society and we all have our own moral principles that we were either taught by life experience or by books. Since every nation has different economy, culture and law, including business culture and standards, one may be faced with unusual situations and different ethical business requirements in different countries. (By Holly Smith, "What Ethical Dilemmas May Be Encountered While Working in Foreign Countries?")

According to Holly Smith the most common ethical dilemmas are bribes, political affairs and illegal activities.

International companies are confronted with a variety of decisions that create ethical dilemmas for the decision makers. "Right–wrong", "just–unjust" derive their meaning and true value from the attitudes of a given culture. Some ethical standards are culture-specific, and one should not be surprised to find that an act that is considered quite ethical in one culture may be looked upon with disregard in another.

Ethical issues concerning bribes

International businesses may be faced with a difficult situation of being involved in corruption without even knowing it sometimes. In some cultures it is acceptable to offer bribes to get a certain business transaction done. Bribery may come in many forms such as money, flowers, gifts, favors and entertainment. Giving any sort of bribe is illegal and unethical in the United States and the UK. However, in some countries there is no other way of getting any business done other than offering bribes. Also, giving a gift in appreciation to someone is considered as a bribe in United States, but it is a normal act in Romania, and a business expense which can be written off in Germany or part of a prime cost in Japan. In Romania, bribery is by law illegal.

The bribe goes by different names in different countries. It is called *mordida* in Mexico, *dash* in South Africa, *baksheesh* for a tip or gratuity in India, Pakistan and in the Middle East, *Schimengeld* for grease money in Germany, and *bastarella* (a little envelope) in Italy. In Romania it is known as *şpagă*. Many business people believe that bribes are necessary costs of doing business in another country. This may be the hardest ethical dilemma you have to face. Although there is a law in the US and in the UK called Foreign Corrupt Practices Act which prevents paying bribes to foreign governments and businesses, it is not certain that the law is strictly followed in other countries.

Take the following example: The Romanian state—owned company Oil Terminal, the largest oil products transport operator in Constanţa harbor, spent tens of thousands of Euros on jewelery, vintage wines, women's handbags and a gold watch between 2009 and 2011 (revealed by a recent Economy Ministry audit). Oil Terminal spent some EUR 6,000 on jewelery, EUR 1,900 for a gold watch, EUR 2,600 on perfumes, some EUR 2,400 on women's handbags, EUR 5,300 on vintage wines. An additional unjustified expenditure of almost EUR 200,000 paid in a contract with a law firm was also discovered during the audit at Oil Terminal. And Oil terminal is not alone.

It is uncertain whether these expenses were simply bribes, or whether the management made personal purchases from the company's money, which is another ethical dilemma in itself. Which one do you think was at play in this case?

What are the factors that push businesses to pay bribes (*șpagas*):

— Competitors are giving bribes to obtain business (which can cause the misuse of the country's resources).

— The pressure for higher levels of performance by top management and shareholders.

— This is an accepted practice in the host country.

— Tax laws of the country encourage bribery. It can be written off as a business expense.

— Government control over business activities.

— Government officials are poorly paid and use bribery to supplement salaries.

— Bureaucratic delays can be costly for business.

— Pressure from politicians to make contributions to political parties or causes.

Ethical issues and political affairs

In many countries, political officials are deeply involved in commercial businesses. You may not even be able to work there without knowing someone in the government. In a country where the government is heavily corrupted, the officials expect to be befriended and bribed. International businesses could gain advantages by offering bribes to government officials. However, it puts other companies at a disadvantage and is an unfair practice of business.

Ethical issues concerning illegal activities

When working in another country, it might be easy to forget your moral standards and fall into the greed of making profit without any limitations. Sometimes if people aren't held responsible for their actions, it could make them become careless about other countries' resources, environment and people. Polluting the country's environment, not following standard employment practices, and evading taxes are all unethical and illegal. However, when everyone else around you is doing all these illegal activities you feel like you will never be held accountable for your actions if you also commit these acts.

I will give you yet another local example. Take the campaign against the cyanide mining at Roşia Montană, which was one of the largest campaigns over a non-political cause in the last 20 years in Romania. Organizations spoke out against the project, from Greenpeace to the Romanian Academy. However, in late 2009, the Romanian government announced that starting the project was a priority and signed a deal with the Romanian-Australian businessman Frank Timiş. The mining license for Roşia Montană was transferred to the Roşia Montană Gold Corporation (RMGC). RMGC is owned 80 percent by Timiş's Toronto-listed company Gabriel Resources, 19.3 percent by the Romanian government via Minvest, and 0.7 percent by local businessmen. RMGC plan to replace the old workings with a new operation according to EU standards, which would be the largest opencast gold mine in Europe. The controversy surrounding this project brought Roşia Montană to the world's attention, as the project never started. The Romanian Government never gave it all the needed approvals, while the Roşia Montană Gold Corporation advertised heavily in the media to gain public support.

What do you think about this example, do you think it involves business ethics or the lack of?

What we must realize is that what may be deemed ethical in our own country is not necessarily deemed as ethical in another country. This often makes conducting global business quite hard. At one time, because we did not have the Internet, it was more of a question of not accidentally disrespecting on another's customs and traditions. However, today, there is much more at stake. You must also not trample all over other businesses—or countries—ethical code, while you remain true to your own businesses or country's ethical code.

A separate attention should be given to the example of an Arabic bank in Romania, or, to be exact, to the trial to open and Arabic bank in Romania.

On February 18, 2008 there was an opening ceremony at JW Marriott hotel, Bucharest, of the first Arabic bank in Romania—Doha Bank from Qatar. But due to the crisis and specific market conditions the Bank is no longer operating here.

Islamic Finance or Baking system has some specific features like *murabahah* (specific sale of goods by installments when the bank buys the asset and then resells it to a person who will use it but at a higher price which a buyer has to pay for it over several years), *Bai' al 'inah* (sale and buy-back agreement), *Bai' bithaman ajil* (deferred payment sale), *Bai' muajjal* (credit sale), *ijara* (redeemable lease when a person uses the asset in exchange for a predetermined number of months or years, and tt the end, he or she can pay cash to own it), *wakalah* (power of attorney) and *sukuk* (islamic bonds) transactions, and also other Islamic financing structures, including *musharakah* (when larger transactions may be arranged as a joint venture where one partner puts up the money and the other puts up the expertise. The partner providing the financing is paid out of the transaction's profits and doesn't receive any money until the project generates cash), *wadiah* (safekeeping), *mudarabah* (Islamic partnership), etc. (definitions are taken from Wikipedia).

On the savings side, Islamic banks offer accounts that share the profits the bank makes from its financing activities. Instead of paying depositors money earned from interest on loans or bond holdings like in Western banks, an Islamic bank distributes its profits at a rate agreed to when the account is opened. If the bank doesn't have profits, it doesn't pay on these accounts; the depositor is expected to share the risk of those receiving the financing. Although these accounts function much like interest-bearing saving accounts and certificates of deposit, the differences are critical to some customers, especially because not all customers qualify for deposit insurance.

In most of the world banking is all about interest. The basic principle of Islamic banking is based on risk-sharing which is a component of trade rather than risk-transfer which we see in the conventional banking. Islamic banking introduces concepts such as profit sharing *(Mudharabah),* safekeeping *(Wadiah),* joint venture *(Musharakah),* cost plus *(Murabahah),* and leasing *(Ijar).* And here the Dilemma comes as under Sharia law, Muslims may not pay or receive interest, a practice known in Arabic as *riba,* so financial services operate a bit differently. Islamic banking (or participant banking) is an activity that is consistent with the principles of Sharia law through the development of Islamic economics. Sharia prohibits the fixed or floating payment or acceptance of specific interest or fees (known also as usury) for loans of money. Investing in businesses that provide goods or services considered contrary to Islamic principles is also *haraam* ("sinful and prohibited").

In an Islamic mortgage transaction, instead of loaning the buyer money to purchase the item, a bank might buy the item itself from the seller, and re-sell it to the buyer at a profit, while allowing the buyer to pay the bank by installments. However, the bank's profit cannot be made explicit and therefore there are no additional penalties for late payment.

This example with an Arabic bank in Romania is more representative for cultural differences in doing business abroad, while other cases (about Oil Terminal and Roșia Montană) show the sensitivity of local business standards.

What companies can do to integrate ethics and business conduct:

Top management must be committed to the company's ethics program. Top management involvement is essential!

A written company code that clearly communicates management's expectations must be developed. The code must be explicit in stating management's intent.

Provide an organizational identity to the ethics program. There should be strong organizational support for a company's ethics program (for example, a high-level ethics committee at the board of directors level as well as at different organizational levels).

A formal program must be in place to implement the ethics code. Every employee must be made to go through a formal training program that teaches employees the ethical code of the company.

Training in ethics must be done not only by intercultural consultants but also by the line managers as role models. Each line manager must be aware of his/her own responsibilities in creating a culture of ethical norms that will be strictly adhered to.

Strict enforcement of codes is essential. Those who violate the company code ought to be punished.

Actions speak louder than words. It is not what a company code or what a company's top management and line managers say but what they actually do in their decisions and actions on behalf of the company that counts.

What other examples of lack of business ethics in Romania you can give? Why do you think they occurred, was it caused by a cultural difference?

This material was based on the following works and articles, which can be recommended for further reading:

1. Arvind V. Phatak, *International Management. Concepts and cases,* South Western College Publishing; Chapter 15, Cincinnati, Ohio, 1996

2. Holly Smith, *What Ethical Dilemmas May Be Encountered While Working in Foreign Countries?*

3. Jed A. Reay, *Global Business and Ethics.*

28. Intercultural communication: Business networking and cultural behavior patterns

Business networking is part of the Romanian business culture. It helps to build new relationships and generate business opportunities. How do business people fulfill this need in Romania?

Business networking is a socioeconomic activity by which groups of business people recognize, create, or act upon business opportunities. It allows business people to build new business relationships and generate business opportunities at the same time. Many business people see business networking as a more cost-effective method of generating new business than advertising or public relations efforts because business networking is a low-cost activity that involves personal commitment rather than company money.

The ability to network—to develop contacts and personal connections with a variety of people—is an important skill for any global business leader. The only obstacle here is that global networking can be extremely difficult when the rules for networking vary across cultures. And these cultural challenges can be so strong that some global leaders often try to avoid networking opportunities— despite how important these opportunities can be for their careers.

How is networking affected by different cultural behavior patterns?

Imagine yourself at a networking event where recruitment agencies, companies and candidates meet. When you see a potential employer from a company you're interested in, you approach the person, look into his or her face, and say the following:

"Hello, I know you are from BCR. I'm very interested in working for BCR and would like to present myself."

A group of foreign professionals in Romania were asked whether according to Romanian business and cultural norms, the person's statement was:

(a) Too direct; (b) Not direct enough; (c) Direct but respectful

The same question was asked to a group of Romanian professionals, and the answers from the two groups were different.

Foreign professionals answered (c), that the statement was respectfully direct, and it was a reasonable way to begin a networking conversation in the United States.

The foreign professionals from other countries, on the other hand, saw the situation quite differently. A few with multicultural experience agreed with the Americans. However, the large majority of foreign businessmen living in Romania chose (a)—that the behavior was too direct and very assertive or aggressive for a Romanian networking event.

According to Romanian behavior patterns the presentation in a soft manner would be more appropriate: "Hello, sir. My name is Adrian Popescu. I am very honored to meet you. Would it be possible for me to introduce myself to you?"

The foreign business people were asked again to evaluate the appropriateness of this statement according to Romanian business and cultural norms: in particular, whether the statement was:

(a) Appropriately polite: When talking with someone at a networking event, especially someone senior to you in either age or professional background, it is important to be highly respectful.

(b) Too polite: Even when talking with someone senior to you in age or professional background, it is important not to be overly polite. It makes you look like you lack confidence and professionalism.

Here the opinions were divided: foreign business people from the US chose (b), whereas business people from Europe chose (a)—that the statement was appropriately polite for this situation in Romania.

A Romanian IT engineer described his experience participating at a multicultural networking event as follows: "I feel that I am performing like a clown, trying to become somebody that I am not, being artificial and fake. During this networking event I want to sell myself, pouring a story about my abilities on a stranger pushing myself to feel like I am doing things to achieve my objectives at all cost."

Here are some areas where cultural differences might step in:

Business card etiquette

Exchanging business cards is an essential part of most cultures. It can be a business ceremony when a business card (as an extension of an individual) is presented to the other person with the front side facing upwards toward the recipient. Offering the card with both hands holding the top corners of the card demonstrates respect to the other person. It's truly an extension of the individual and is treated with respect. Things like tucking it into a pocket after receiving it, writing on it, bending or folding it in any way, or even looking at it again after you've first accepted it and looked at it aren't considered polite and can insult your fellow Asian networker, for example.

How are business cards treated in Romania? What do you think, based on your experience?

Consideration of "Personal Space."

It's crucial to understand the subtle, unspoken dynamics of personal space in every culture. Some cultural dynamics are fine with close, personal inter-action, while others demand a bigger distance. This is not a point to underestimate.

There are three basic separations to consider when taking personal space into account. For Americans, they typically are: public, social and personal space.

In Saudi Arabia, their social space equates to our intimate space, in the Netherlands, this might be reversed due to the fact that their personal space equates to our social space. Do your homework and be sensitive to cultural differences in this area.

How can global business professionals acquire this critical global leadership skill—networking?

Three pieces of advice can be given for success in learning how to adapt behavior across cultures in a networking event or in any other situation where you need to switch your cultural behavior in order to be effective in a new cultural environment.

(1) Learn from local people: Watch carefully how others operate in networking situations, and learn what behaviors should be applied or should not be even considered. Customize your own approach from what you observe to develop a style that feels appropriate to you, and that is also effective in the new setting.

(2) Try to understand the new cultural logic: Learn the concept for the new behavior from the perspective of the new culture. For example, why "small talk" is such an important part of networking or why direct eye contact is necessary, or how close you should be standing to a person next to you, should you have a smiling face while talking or serious tone of your voice is more suitable during this presentation and... do you shake hands or not? Understand from the Romanian point of view why and how you should

speak positively about yourself and your qualifications. Master the logic of the new culture and the behavior and you will feel much more comfortable to perform in this cultural environment.

(3) Practice many times, and in situations that are stressful and create the pressure of real situations. Then local networking behavior will be so deeply integrated into your mind that it becomes your "new normal" networking pattern— something you do naturally.

If you have the ability to consult with someone in that country who's familiar with that culture before interacting with their businesspeople, do it.

This advice can help you to master networking in any culture as this method can be applied to any other global leadership situation you might face.

You can read more about this subject in these articles:

"Networking Etiquette around the world" by Ivan Misner and "How to Network across cultures by Andy Molinsky," HBR blog Network.

29. Intercultural communications: corporate holiday parties in Romania

This story covers the struggles of organizing holiday celebrations in a multi-cultural corporate environment, while keeping everyone in the company happy.

Being at the height of corporate Christmas Party season which style will you choose for celebration?

It is a Christmas party in Romania (like in many European countries and in the US), it can be Hannukah in Israel or New Year Party in Russia. This is the easiest part—to celebrate the holiday with the company team according to the local traditions. What if your staff members come from different countries and you, as a manager, have to recognize this and please them all?

The holidays seem to bring diversity issues to the discussions about which celebrations to recognize—or not—and sometimes create conflict as people's deeply rooted beliefs about the individual versus the group, touch upon people's identities, precious traditions, and sense of the sacred. The ensuing clashes, complications and confusion can lead organizations to cancel holiday celebrations all together.

Is this approach the most effective response to the inevitable conflicts that occur?

Recently I had a client who approached me for help with communication issues within the company; after talking with the staff and conducting a survey, I identified some employee morale issues among the organization's challenges. One big issue was that leadership took away any mention or expression of any holidays to "avoid offending." This was not in response to any incident; it was introduced without a dialogue with the staff. The organization is a social service agency providing humanitarian aid, whose staff does difficult work for disabled people; so the many festivities around Halloween, Christmas, etc. had been real "light spots" in the life of deprived people and provided much-needed fun and important bonding for the staff.

Another example that can be given here; a new manager overseeing a department that was key in providing language and culture training services to a foreign organization here in Romania noticed a few small groups in the company—the religious minorities. Christian, a Buddhist and a Jehovah's Witness were completely separated from the Arabic influence. The manager had a feeling that this marginalization was symptomatic of a general trend of not really hearing or engaging "the others" which was problematic for a company dedicated to bridging differences. With the help of the outsourced expert four months ago, a dialogue was opened on how they could create a holiday celebration that was more inclusive of the traditions in the company and something everyone could participate in (ex., the Jehovah's Witness was never able to participate in any holiday celebrations, birthdays, etc). This created a clash because the Christians, which made up the majority of the group, felt they had an obligation and a right to be able to celebrate Jesus' birth, and doing anything else felt like they were denying that or taking the "real" meaning away from the occasion. In the end, a very nice party was organized, but only a third of the employees attended, since it wasn't "mandatory to attend."

These stories can illustrate extreme positions of organizations—"doing" diversity and inclusion can be HARD work, and many companies lack the time, will, and the especially skills, to do this work and have these conversations.

The first company in my story had good intentions, but took the easy way out of a hard, potentially messy conversation with staff in which they could have explored (in a collaborative way) possible approaches, solutions, and alternatives.

The second company did not have enough time to build up sufficient trust and positive relationships with staff to suggest such a change.

To sum up, the conflict over holidays isn't necessarily the actual problem, but one symptom of our fear or struggles to think creatively and problem solve together. Shutting down the conversation doesn't make it easier or make it go away. It makes it go subconscious where things get much trickier to deal with.

Diversity and inclusion should enrich, not sterilize. It should expand, not constrict. It should say "both/and" instead of "either/or."

People are hungry for meaning in their lives and work, and holidays and celebrations are a vital way for people to bond, celebrate, and find satisfaction. Taking away the sacred does not enrich, expand, or "both and." It's an ineffective approach to pluralism... and to fear.

Happy New Year!

30. Intercultural communication: Frugal or reverse innovation. Doing more with less in a cross-cultural approach

As I was doing some research on Frugal or Reverse Innovation, I recently came across an interesting and powerful example in a Harvard Business Review article, written by Pr. Vijay Govindarajan from the Tuck School of Business at Dartmouth. Before delving into "doing more with less," let's follow the example of French car producer Renault and its Romanian brand Dacia.

Romanian Cars from a French Company on the German Autobahn: "Dacia is a Romanian car manufacturer acquired in 1999 by French automaker Renault with the aim of designing low-cost passenger vehicles for emerging Eastern European markets. The

Logan, a five-seater with a spacious trunk, was introduced in Romania in 2004 and subsequently to neighboring countries. The Logan's basic version, costing €5,000, was revolutionary in the automotive industry. In Germany alone, where the car is offered starting at €8,000, Dacia's sales jumped from about 6,000 units in 2006 to about 85,000 units in 2009—this in a land studded with its own car brands. To offer the car at such low prices, Renault followed a stringent design-to-cost approach. The Logan consists of fewer parts than the average Western car and is made of traditional steel in a labor-intensive assembly process in a low-cost country. To meet the needs of emerging market customers, the car has a fuel filter, increased ground clearance, and a battery that can survive extreme weather conditions. Maintenance is simple; a basic technician can do the work. Interestingly, the Logan originally was conceived at Renault's French R&D headquarters. Product development responsibility gradually shifted to the company's new R&D center in Romania."

International companies looking for expansion have shifted their focus to emerging markets. But if they want to succeed in these markets companies must understand that they will have to change their approach to innovation.

For most companies in Western markets, innovation means the development of new products with more advanced resources. But in emerging markets, where their products must appeal to the millions who don't have millions, companies will need to apply frugal or reverse innovation when this innovation drives down the price to a level that economically disadvantaged consumers feel is affordable. This affordability is also backed up by state-of-the-art quality.

Frugal innovation means to generate considerably more business and social value while significantly reducing the use of scarce resources. It's about solving—and even transcending—the paradox of "doing more with less."

Carlos Ghosn, the CEO of the Renault-Nissan Alliance, coined the term "frugal engineering" in 2006—inspired by Indian engineers' ability to innovate cost-effectively (and swiftly) under extreme resource constraints. As Ghosn points out: "In the West, when we face huge problems and we lack resources, we tend to give up (too) easily. Frugal Innovation is about never giving up!" Under Ghosn's leadership, Renault-Nissan has proactively adopted frugal engineering—and the underlying mindset—and established itself as a major global manufacturer of both low-cost vehicles as well as electric cars—two of the fastest growing segments in the global automotive market.

After being launched in Romania by Renault in 2004 Logan became Renault's cash cow across recession-hit European markets as well as in many emerging economies. And Carlos Ghosn, the CEO of the Renault-Nissan Alliance, wants to do more. In 2012, he dispatched Gérard Detourbet, a senior executive from Paris who was running Renault's entry-level car business, to India. From his new base in Chennai, Detourbet will design and build a "global small car"—a €3,500 vehicle that will first be launched in India and then introduced in Brazil and South Africa. You can bet that when Detourbet returns to Renault's headquarters in Paris, he will bring with him the frugal mindset.

Dacia is a Romanian car manufacturer acquired in 1999 by French automaker Renault with the aim of designing low-cost passenger vehicles for emerging Eastern European markets. The Logan, a five-seater with a spacious trunk, was introduced in Romania in 2004 and subsequently to neighboring countries. The Logan's basic version, costing US$6,500, was revolutionary in the automotive industry well before the Tata Nano appeared on the scene. Dacia now offers pickups, vans, station wagons, and mini SUVs in emerging as well as developed markets. In Germany alone, where the car is offered starting at US$9,400, Dacia's sales jumped from about 6,000 units in 2006 to about 85,000 units in 2009—this in a land studded with its own car brands.

To offer the car at such low prices, Renault followed a stringent design-to-cost approach. The Logan consists of fewer parts than the average Western car and is made of traditional steel in a labor-intensive assembly process in a low-cost country. To meet the needs of emerging market customers, the car has a fuel filter, increased ground clearance, and a battery that can survive extreme weather conditions. Maintenance is simple; a basic technician can do the work. Interestingly, the Logan originally was conceived at Renault's French R&D headquarters. Product development responsibility gradually shifted to the company's new R&D center in Romania.

Dacia launched Logan in Germany following **five principles** that may be useful to other companies planning to bring emerging market products into developed markets.

Focus on building concepts, not products. Concepts can be scaled up or down for global markets. For the German market, Dacia scaled up the product concept with more safety features and more appealing exterior characteristics, such as metallic paint which allowed the automaker to charge higher prices and higher profit margins.

Select target customers. Customers are people who buy Logan instead of a used car, a cheap, Asian import, or a very small European car valuing price, space, and reliability.

Low cost but not low quality. Dacia's marketing strategy was built on the fact that it was able to offer low prices without sacrificing quality and safety.

Commercial innovations are essential. The Logan is not just a product innovation, but a commercial innovation as well. Dacia employs low-cost marketing—no TV commercials. Initially cars were sold through existing Renault dealerships.

Protect global brand. In order to avoid potential negative effects on the core brand Renault introduced Dacia Logan as a separate brand.

The Jugaad mindset was applied to Frugal innovation. Jugaad is a Hindi word meaning "an improvised solution born from ingenuity": Seek opportunity in adversity, do more with less, think and act flexibly, keep it simple, include the margin and follow your heart. You can read about Jugaad in "Jugaad: A

Frugal, Flexible Approach to Innovation" written by Navi Radjou, Jaideep Prabhu and Simone Ahuja.

What is your opinion? Do you have more examples?

31. Intercultural: Learning from Ireland's Celtic Tiger while preparing for St. Patrick's Day

The upcoming Irish National Day gives some food for some thoughts—the ties between Romania and Ireland and highlights what brings the two nations together, and what sets them apart.

It was Ireland's turn to head the Council of the EU (for a seventh time) as of the beginning of 2013, and it was quite a timely choice. In 2013 Ireland marks 40 years of EU membership, which can serve as a very good illustration to what the EU can do with countries that know precisely what they need and have the will to pursue it.

It is still too early to tell whether the Celtic Tiger, as Ireland was known before the crisis, is coming back in the sense that was meant then—with dynamic growth and dropping unemployment. The Celtic Tiger, however, can be recognized also in the successful example of the austerity program that delivers. The power of the Tiger can be seen also in Ireland's determination to cash down its membership in the EU for the past 40 years. Ireland has radically changed and it looks different for the better. So, Fáilte, Éire! For the seventh time.

There is something in Irish development that Romania definitely stands to learn from. Celtic Tiger refers to the economy of the Republic of Ireland between 1995 and 2008, a period of rapid economic growth. This was a period of growing interest in Ireland and its people. The organization of large-scale celebrations of the national day—St. Patrick's Day, March 17—abroad was made possible by the destruction of the negative stereotypes about the Irish nation and the increased interest in Irish culture. The upcoming St. Patrick's Day promotes Irish national confidence and causes a further increase in international popularity of Irish culture. In Romania too the Irish community celebrates the National Day with a ball which will be in its second edition this year.

Saint Patrick is a national Saint Hero of the country, whose name is associated with various legends. Two of them are quite well-known today. People believe that it was St Patrick who helped to get rid Ireland of snakes—luring them into the sea. It is true that there are no snakes on this island (although biologists say they've never been there). Another legend says that Patrick used the shamrock to explain the concept of the Holy Trinity to pagans, three leaves on one stem representing the one but three idea of God. That's why nowadays, the Irish people pin this ornament on St. Patrick's Day as a national symbol.

Until the mid-1990s, the celebration of St. Patrick's Day was spread mainly among Irish emigrants in the large Irish Diaspora. At the turn of the millennium, the celebration of the national Saint of Ireland was first organized in many European and Asian countries, such as Germany, France, Russia, Denmark, Norway, Italy, Spain, Japan, China, Singapore, Malaysia, Hong Kong, South Korea.

Most of the activities on St. Patrick's Day are organized by the Government of Ireland and the various Irish companies and organizations: The Ireland Funds, Culture Ireland, Irish Network. A distinctive feature of the international success of St. Patrick's Day is the fact that Irish people actively seek to include the local population in the festivities. The Irish communities act as hospitable hosts of the festival, willingly offering guests to make their own contributions.

In Romania, there is the Ireland Romania Network, which organizes the St. Patrick's Ball. There is also the Irish Embassy in Bucharest, which has been functional since 2005. The historical ties between Romania and Ireland don't date back too long, the diplomatic relations between Romania and Ireland were established only in April 1990, and since May 20, 1994, Romania has had an embassy in Dublin.

Bucharest is one of the few capitals in the world where the Irish community is not very large, but the influence of the Irish community here has nothing to do with its size, rather it is the rapid growth of Irish business, despite the fact that the local economy is experiencing significant difficulties.

The most picturesque presence of Ireland in Bucharest can be seen in the middle of March, on St. Patrick's Day, where the growing Irish business community uses this opportunity to express itself.

The success of Irish business in Romania and the growing popularity of the event could be attributed simply to the account of "Irish luck." But Irish business people comment that they are very similar to Romanian people because of the same sense of humor. A good example is the breaking new musical ground—an album "Voices From The Merry Cemetery" composed by Shaun Davey, the well-known Irish composer, who has been working with Irish and Romanian musicians.

Many Irish traditional values seem to be common for Romanians: rural simplicity, vision and imagination, romance and idealism, irony and sense of humor, informality, poetic tendencies, love of literature, music, theatre, warmth and charm, social anchors of land, church, family... St. Patrick's Day celebrations have brought all these values together! Irish people have a reputation for ease and elegance of speech and a readiness to put things into practice.

They tend to have a more flexible approach to organization than, for example, British people. This is reflected in the importance given to personal relationships, similarly to Romanian people, a talent for improvisation and a dislike of rigid systems and bureaucracy. Irish people are essentially cooperative and work well in teams. Teams will commonly accept collective responsibility for decisions and implementations.

Sounds encouraging for all mixed Romanian-Irish teams, doesn't it? What's your experience with working or socializing with Irish people? And if you're Irish, how has it been to work/socialize with Romanians?

32. Intercultural: The dual-culture phenomenon in international organizations

Lets meet a bi-cultural manager currently doing business in Romania and take the story further to illustrate the importance of knowing how to deal with bi-cultural team members.

More and more managers within international companies have a dual-cultural background! Recently I had a chance to interview a director of an American company doing business in Romania. During our conversation about different cultural experiences which she dealt with as a child and a teenager, Maria, the Director of Sales (Europe) of a large US oil equipment company based in Romania—where the company has its European headquarters—acknowledged that she had several cultural conflicts. These conflicts were not imposed by the external environment but by her personal development and personal values connected to cultural roots, her identity or, to be exact, by the complexity of these roots.

At the end of our 6-hour conversation, she confessed that she was worried about her business trip to Saudi Arabia as a member of the sales team. With parents from different cultures—a Korean father and a Serbian mother—she had spent her teenage years in the US. She did not speak Korean, but was fluent in Serbian and English. Equipped with an MBA from a leading American business school, she had successfully negotiated sales around the US. However, when she got married to a man from Lebanon and spent several years in the Middle East, Maria was uncertain about her business status due to the current situation in Saudi Arabia, a country she knew little about. She is currently located in Romania, where women-leaders in top management is not a forbidden concept, but in Saudi Arabia women have very limited access to the public and almost no access to business management positions.

A week later after our meeting, she called me to express her surprise as quite quickly and easily she had become a mediator in business negotiations, not only for her own team members but for the Saudis as well.

Not many organizations today that employ dual-cultural persons are aware of their knowledge and skills and confuse ethnicity with country specific understanding. For example, Maria might be better at understanding and operating across multiple cultural contexts, rather than representing a Korean cultural context, as she never lived in Korea and is only partially familiar with it. Similar mistakes may make it difficult for bi-cultural employees to contribute their most important abilities and, at the same time, increase the personal insecurities that many bi-cultural people might feel.

The success of international companies and organizations is based more and more on the transfer and sharing of information, knowledge across organizational and cultural boundaries. As collaboration, communication and trust building gain importance, and, as flows of knowledge and processes become increasingly more critical success factors, the role of individuals in mediating between and within cultures becomes vital for business performance.

Bi-cultural individuals, like Maria, are people who have internalized more than one cultural profile, and represent a growing and under explored group, which is particularly important in the context of international organizations. As a result of the increasing number of mixed marriages and foreign-born and second generation immigrants, there are more and more people today and in the nearest future with bi-cultural or mixed cultural profiles. These individuals carry with them mixed cultural identities: they possess the obvious knowledge of their own cultures and unique skills that do not belong to mono-cultural individuals.

It is important here to show the difference between cultural identification and cultural knowledge. A person can have knowledge of another culture without identifying with it. For example, international students, expats and even tourists may be able to acquire knowledge about a different culture and apply this knowledge to adjust their behavior, without actively identifying with that culture. Cultural identification involves answering the question: "Who am I?" with reference to a particular set of values, attitudes, beliefs and behavioral assumptions.

Bi-cultural persons have more than one cultural frame which can be applied in response to different situations. Because of their inner cultural conflict they are more systematic and careful in processing these complex cultural situations resulting in more complex cultural representations. They may have developed certain skills that allow them to better deal with the demands of today's dynamic complex cultural situations.

Maria, for example, may be successful in Saudi Arabia, not because she has some cultural knowledge of Saudi Arabia, but because she has had to confront and manage the differences in her Korean and Serbian identities living in the US, which has allowed her to develop higher order cognitive skills that are not specific to any of her cultural schemes.

Today, global business success for international companies depends not only on being effective in understanding and bridging between different cultures, but also on being inter-culturally effective, meaning to integrate diverse cultural knowledge even further. Having these unique skills, bi-cultural individuals may be the ones to provide the type of integration and mediation required. They may be the best as boundary spanners in multicultural teams, bridge between organizational units in culturally different contexts, or be catalysts for creativity and innovation because of their cognitive complexity.

Thus, what are the intercultural skills for the benefits they bring—benefits that carry significant monetary value to employers:

- Keeping teams running efficiently
- Good for reputation of the company

– Bringing in new clients and building trustful relationships with them

- Communicating with overseas partners
- Able to work with diverse colleagues
- Increased productivity
- Increased sales

The organizational cultures within companies, in which the cultural diversity is the goal to be achieved, should accept the fact that cultural diversity exists within individuals and is recognized in the same way as the cultural diversity between individuals and is considered to be a valuable asset for organizations.

(This interesting topic has been addressed in 2009–2010 by Mary Yoko Brannen, Visiting Professor of Strategy, INSEAD Business School and David C. Thomas, Professor of International Management, Director of the Centre for Global Workforce Strategy, Segal Graduate School of Business, Simon Fraser University, Vancouver, BC, Canada).

33. "The Connoisseurs of Life: distinctive properties around the world and Romanian owners"

"Built on centuries of tradition and dedicated to innovation, the Sotheby's International Realty brand artfully unites connoisseurs of life with their aspirations through a deeply connected global network of exceptional people." (Sotheby's International Realty's description of their own services)

In the world of luxury real estate this company has its leading position due to many factors: unique history, experienced leadership, extraordinary marketing, etc.

Its motto—"Artfully uniting extraordinary homes with extraordinary lives"—brings properties and its owners immediately to the top level of the luxury niche in the world's real estate market.

It brings the style of life combined with the international exposure and taste of art—metropolitan, mountain, waterfront, wine &vineyards, ski, retirement, historic, country living.

How this brand can fit into Romanian real estate market?

Through the partnership with the local leading real estate company.

X Real Estate, the largest real estate consulting company with Romanian capital, offers the public the opportunity to acquire buildings that once were enlivened by famous national figures.

Famous properties are part of the special property portfolio promoted by X Real Estate. "Lux means exclusivity and uniqueness. A dwelling located in a unique location will always have a higher price, just as it does in the case of an artwork—because there are not two of them!" explained President of X Real Estate.

"In over 23 years of activity in selling and renting premium properties, company's leadership is pioneering both in the trading of heritage buildings and the office space segment, buildings of a great historical and cultural value, former residences of famous families of Cantacuzino, Ghika, Vintilă Brătianu and the scientist Nicolae Paulescu," said President of X Real Estate.

Besides the historical buildings built at the end of 19th—beginning of the 20th centuries, whose ideal destination is embassies and companies representative offices, X Real Estate has in its portfolio also residential properties, both classical and modern.

Now comes the important question—how to apply the patterns and standards of the international real estate market to the local market with its local specifics in Romania? How the international and the local leading real estate players can create a Romanian brand with the international recognition?

"Luxury attracts more luxury. The prices of the luxury market are not fuelled entirely by the external influences but also by the consumption habits of local entrepreneurs. Then, the value of the luxury residential properties will likely follow the evolution of luxury goods and not the overall residential property prices" said Bonnie Stone Sellers, CEO of International Real Estate Division of Christie's, Sotheby's competitor.

Luxury home sales have grown spectacularly over the past 5 years and have come to account for 5 percent of the total housing market. High-income Romanians and expatriates leading multinational companies are the main buyers.

About 30% of the properties available for sale on the luxury segment are listed at prices of over one million Euros, according to X Real Estate. The latest trend noted in this segment is buyers' desire to acquire properties already built by architects and designers to move to the new home as quickly as possible.

While clients buying property in Bucharest are interested in either historic buildings or modern buildings but located in the central areas of the city, customers looking for villas outside the capital prefer properties located on the shores of one of the lakes around Bucharest. The luxury waterfront places are the Snagov, Buftea, and Mogoşoaia lakes.

Nearly a quarter of those interested in buying luxury properties are primarily interested in investing in them to increase their value and then resell them at a significantly higher price, in the context of the luxury real estate market being on an upward trend.

Looks like lifestyle is common keywords for both companies—a large inventory of luxury homes that match your lifestyle choices such as waterfront, golf, island, vacation, mountain and many others.

What else Romania can gain in this case:

– Economic growth due to the potential investors' awareness of the International player presence in Romania;

– International exposure of Romanian properties;

– Stronger access for international investors to the local luxury properties;

– Restructuring of the local real estate market according to the international requirements as the luxury level becomes more visible and approachable as a lifestyle.

The luxury real estate market in Romania has several features that differentiate it from the developed markets but fits into the local picture. Investment threshold begins lower and acquisitions are still dictated by snobbery. "I buy a villa in the X area because others have bought there or because it is trendy to have a home there. But the crisis has changed attitudes and the premium market. Customers are more cautious. It is interesting that in this luxury niche Romania has recently registered purchases made by citizens from the former Soviet space", says the economist. How did they get here?

Most of them have businesses in Romania and prefer to stay in a residence rather than in a hotel. Until a few years ago, this category of customers made luxury real estate purchases in expensive markets: Great Britain, France or Switzerland. And, like global trends in the market of luxury-apartment show, the areas of migration of the rich will trigger investment opportunities with a short term return of investments through rent. Is Romanian next? Why not?

There are investment opportunities in this market. Most of them prefer to place their money in unique historic properties or properties with special architecture. Bucharest has enough historical buildings completely refurbished for sale. And their number and the dynamic of acquisitions already define a niche of the luxury real estate in Romania. It is a type of investment that does not necessarily yield immediate seeking for rent; they buy an asset that can be converted into cash later.

The globalization of business opportunities, industrialized production and cultural attractions have created a set of major cities that function as a network. The global urban centers have distinct attractions and an easiness of doing business. These attributes act like a magnet for mobile professionals and entrepreneurs, whose number is increasing constantly.

One more pitfall—Cultural differences!

First one—the level of readiness of the local market. While the international clients have been already educated by Sotheby's International Realty quality and standards, local Romanian customers need some adaptation to their new image of a luxury customer with luxury expectations and luxury lifestyle.

Second one is connected with the balance between the organizational culture of the brand and the national culture of the market.

Which one has greater influence on values and behavior—national culture (NC) or organizational culture (OC)?

The question is important because it leads us to investigate the degree of control that the headquarters of a multinational company can realistically exert on its subsidiary located in Romania.

Are organizational values so powerful? And influence the NC? It is important to know. Because if they ARE, employees of the local company as well customers (potential investors and property buyers) can be conditioned to expressing values that contradict national values. In this case, new brand control over the OC of a foreign-based subsidiary is always insecure.

The evidence is ambiguous. There is no doubt that organizational values do influence in the long term, and generate patterns of uniformity among organizational units, regardless of geographic, functional or business boundaries.

But this does not mean that they operate as deeply as do the values of the NC, or significantly modify the NC when the two are in conflict which influence the main goal—profits!

What can be recommended here? Cultural due diligence!

Cultural due diligence involves steps like: determining the importance of culture, assessing the culture of both—a target and an acquirer. It is useful to know with respect to dimensions such as centralized versus decentralized decision making, speed in decision making, time horizon for decisions, level of team work, management of conflict, risk orientation, openness to change, communication styles, etc.

It is necessary to assess the cultural fit between the brand and local leader based on cultural profile. Potential sources of clash must be managed. It is necessary to identify the impact of cultural gap, and develop and execute strategies to use the information in the cultural profile to assess the impact that the differences have.

The Cultural Assessment starts with asking the right questions:

1. How does cultural integration planning fit into acquisition strategic planning, negotiation, and due diligence processes?

2. How can executives identify critical implementation issues during the planning and negotiation stages?

3. What integration tools are useful for functional departments? For merged cross-functional projects? For individuals and multicultural small task groups who must work together for the first time?

4. What are the roles of top (from one culture) and mid-level (from another culture) management (on both sides) during implementation?

Acknowledge cultural differences but simultaneously create a common corporate culture with a single goal: achieving high performance. Successful cross-border M&As are often those that embrace cultural diversity as a creative and fertile source of positive new "ways of doing things" and go on to create a "third culture" that is shared by all employees and embraced by external stakeholders. Awareness of language, cultural values, attitudes and behaviors are critical success factors of the integration process.

More broadly, the challenges of changing from a single, culturally integrated national organization operating in a familiar market in one time zone to managing a cross-border organizational culture where perspectives and issues can take many management teams by surprise.

Set clear expectations and invest in high-quality, two-way communication. Recognizing and adapting to the different communication styles and expectations of the cultures involved will also help to reduce any feelings of mistrust and concern—not only among employees but, just as importantly, among clients and other stakeholders in the new markets.

Create a role-model within the company culture and the customer will follow!

Sotheby's International Realty made a decision not to come to Romania—the brand was too strong for the developing market.

34. "COM UM QUILO DE CARNE DE VACA E UM LITRO DE VINHO NÂO SE MORRE DE FOME" —Corporate Social Responsibility at the International Level

This saying can be understood and shared by both nations—Romanian and Portuguese.

Portugal is a true and reliable friend of Romania, enjoying much appreciation among its compatriots. The excellent level of current relations is based on the common Latin origin that these peoples share, as well as on a fruitful dialogue and on an increasing cooperation, which cover mainly political, military, economic and cultural aspects.

Portuguese and Romanians share a common cultural and historical matrix that goes back to the origins of the European civilization: Roman Empire. At a first glance, apart from their Latin heritage, Portugal and Romania don't appear to have much in common. Portugal gained its independence nearly nine centuries ago and has been an independent state ever since, having the oldest borders in Europe. The Portuguese created an empire that included territories across the world, thus spreading their culture and language on three continents—Africa, Asia, and South America—it became a multicultural nation. The Romanians, on the other hand, had a different historical destiny. The current territory was divided for centuries into three principalities—Moldavia, Wallachia and Transylvania—under the dominance of either the Ottoman or the Austro-Hungarian Empire. The Unification of 1918 configured the modern independent state, but the further territorial losses which occurred during the Second World War redesigned the map of the Romanian state as it is known today.

These differences have seriously influenced the ways in which the national identity and history have been conceived: while the Portuguese mythologized their glorious past, the Romanians take great pride in claiming that they never fought a battle for conquering, but fighting only to defend their land and defeating superior enemies, such as the Ottoman Empire. Being the last Christian fortress and defending the West against the Muslim invasion is one of the historical myths that created the national Romanian identity.

In Romania the Portuguese are mostly interested in investing in IT, pharma, banking, consulting, real estate, energy and renewable energy. However the dominating presence is in constructions, because Romania needs work on its infrastructure and Portugal is very qualified in this sector.

The economic exchanges between Romania and Portugal have increased constantly in the last years, especially the Portuguese investments in Romania, in construction and energy areas. It is strongly believed that the current situation of Romania—its economic growth, along with the opportunities it provides for the foreign investors—will convince more entrepreneurs from Portugal to see it as an attractive destination.

"We believe that the path to business growth is driven by cultural understanding. Portugal and Romania have a cultural proximity that defies the distance that separate them", said Alain Bonte, who arrived in Romania for business opportunities several years ago and discovered modern Romanian paintings which became his collection.

The general manager of Generalcom, Alain Bonte, has a wide range of business interests in Romania from pharmacies to leasing and real estate rentals.

Listed on the Bucharest Stock Exchange, Generalcom is a company specialized in letting commercial spaces in Bucharest, but with a mixed interest portfolio. This company owns a majority stake in Centrofarm, one of the oldest Romanian pharmacy brands with 38 stores, 80 per cent in Bucharest. Generalcom also acquired traditional medicine chain Plafar in 2007. This is another famous Romanian brand with 80 years on the market and a turnover last year of under a million Euro. The plan this year is to grow this to between two and three million Euro.

Generalcom

Letter of commercial spaces

- Companies: Pharma producer Sintofarm Bucuresti
- Pharmacy chain Centrofarm
- Traditional medicine chain Plafar
- Total Leasing
- Minority shareholder in Global Asigurări

Sonae Sierra

Shopping center developer

- Projects: shopping centers in Craiova, Dolj county; Ploieşti, Prahova county; Parklake Plaza mall in Bucharest in partnership with Caelum

Millennium Bank
- Employees: 500
- Branches: 41
- Planned number by end of 2011: 100

Lena Construcoes: finishing passage near Obor
Mota-Engil Romania
Construction
- Divisions: Civil Engineering & Building Construction, Environment & Services, Transport Concessions, Industry & Energy

Soares da Costa: bidding for Braşov motorway
The list of business projects can be extended...

But business developments are not the only line keeping both countries close to each other.

The cultural dimension is undoubtedly a very important component of the overall relations between two countries, as it reveals so many similarities between these two nations, about the way they experience life, bringing people even closer in thoughts, acts and feelings. "In this respect, the success which the on-going event called '100 years of Romanian painting', organized in Lisbon, has had so far, is remarkable. About 50,000 visitors are estimated to see the exhibition until its closure", commented Alain Bonte.

Bonte Collection is a genuine Romanian modern art gallery, bringing together works by some of the most valuable artists of the nineteenth and twentieth centuries: Nicolae Grigorescu, Gheorghe Petraşcu, Adam Bălţatu, Camil Ressu, Iosif Iser, Theodor Pallady, Nicolae Dărăscu, Francisc Şirato, Alexandru Ciucurencu, Nicolae Vermont, Vasile Popescu, Hippolytus Strâmbu, Kimon Login, Arthur Verona, Dimitrescu Stephen, Stephen Smith, Leo Biju, Theodorescu Sion, Samuel Mützner, Rodica Maniu, Magdalena Rădulescu, Constantin Isachie, Dumitru Ghiaţă, Rudolf Schweitzer-Cumpăna, Jean Cheller. "The work selection is not only a true sample of a collector's passion, but ultimately a rare devotion to a cultural cause and a high faith—practiced while with professional arguments professional—that the Romanian fine arts deserve to be properly known across the national borders as well." (Nine o'Clock, June 10, 2016)

www.ingramcontent.com/pod-product-compliance
Lightning Source LLC
Chambersburg PA
CBHW071601030726
47593CB00001BA/258